rhyming & stealing: a history of the

Beastie Boys

Published in 1998 by
INDEPENDENT MUSIC PRESS LTD

Rhyming & Stealing: A History Of The Beastie Boys
by Angus Batey
All Rights Reserved

British Library Cataloguing-in-Publication Data
A catalogue for this book is available from The British Library

ISBN 1-89-7783-14-0
Printed and bound in the UK
Order No: MR 55672
UPC No. 7 52187 55672 5

Photo Credits: 1, 3, 4: Peter Anderson/SIN; 2: Brendan Beirne/Rex Features;
5: Rex Features ; 6: Andrew Catlin/SIN; 7: Piers Allardyce/SIN;
8, 11: Martyn Goodacre/SIN; 9: Rip/All Action;
10: Steve Double/SIN; 12: Levy/All Action
Front Cover: Richard Beland/SIN; Back Cover: Marina Chavez/SIN
Every effort has been made to correctly acknowledge and credit the photographers herein. However, should any error or omission appear, it is unintentional, and the publisher should be contacted immediately.

Exclusive Distributor for the United States and Canada:

OMNIBUS PRESS
A Division of Music Sales Corporation
257 Park Avenue South
New York, NY 10010 USA

rhyming & stealing: a history of the Beastie Boys

by Angus Batey

Independent Music Press
London

CONTENTS

ACKNOWLEDGEMENTS

There are many people to whom I owe a debt of thanks for their help in getting this book completed. I hope I have remembered them all here.

In particular I would like to thank Jake Barnes, whose attentive reading and perceptive editing of early drafts of some chapters made an immeasurable difference to the quality of the whole. Additionally, his incredible aptitude for all things to do with Apple computers helped save much time and heartache. He truly is the Mac Daddy.

I am also indebted to those people who generously gave their time to be interviewed, all of whom are acknowledged in the text and notes. I would like to make special mention of my gratitude to Bill Adler, no stranger to thankyou sections of hip-hop books. Bill has more hook-ups than an angler's convention and was generous in sharing them.

Several people were kind enough to provide access to source material, some of it previously unpublished. Their input was invaluable. They are Will Ashon, Blade, Stephen Dowling, Paul Houston, Karen Johnson, Ted Kessler and Leo Wyndham, to whom I extend many thanks.

Though they may not have realised, many people have said the right thing at the right time and have therefore helped me overcome the obstacles I am all too adept at placing in my own path. Some discussed the Beasties, hip-hop music or the problems of writing books with me at times when they had a hundred better things to do. Others made tangential but essential contributions that ranged from providing lifts across rural France to listening to my moaning when things were going wrong. They are all great. They are Nazzi Armin, Nihal Arthunayake, Mark Bethell, Gill Burke, Les Carter, Crissi Cromer, Daz Davies, Johnny Dee, Claire Hughes and Johnny,

Stephen Jelbert, Rachel Kennedy, Pete Lawton, Gavin Martin, Martin Millar, John Mulvey, Bob Oscroft, the Scratch crew (Matt, Rob and Hils), Victoria Segal, Rupert Shepherd, Nigel Sloane, Ed Stern, Mark Sutherland's mate Steve, Kevin Thorold, Lisa Verrico, Darren Watts, Ian Watson, Steven Wells, Tessa Wills and Ben Willmott. The whole of the Chomerac World Cup posse were also most generous in their tolerance of my odd behaviour and deserve at the very least a laurel, and hearty handshake. And my parents, Don and Olive Batey, were, as ever, rock-like in their support. As Adam Yauch says somewhere on *Ill Communication*, "I'll give a little shout out to my Dad and Mom/For bringing me into this world, and so on."

Though the book would have been finished quicker without such distractions, I probably would have grown to hate the Beastie Boys and everything to do with them were it not for the makers of the game *Gran Turismo* on the Sony Playstation. Between them and the organisers of France '98 I owe some part of my present sanity, and I feel that their contribution has therefore been invaluable. My publishers, though, may disagree. Vehemently. It is also worth mentioning that during the hectic period spent completing this book I have mostly been eating the fine food supplied by Chicago Pizza - 'Pizza With An Attitude'. And no attitude problem. Cheers.

Last, but by no means least, I wish to thank Martin and Kaye of Independent Music Press. The idea for this book was Martin's, and his continued belief in my ability to write it, coupled with just the right degree of cajoling and emotional blackmail, finally saw it through to completion. Though there have been times during the preparation of the manuscript when I have wanted to kill him, I think I now understand that he was right. I hope you will agree.

Angus Batey
Tulse Hill, South London, July 1998

THE SCOOBY DOO INTRODUCTION

No-one noticed the silver disc as it stole silently across the south London skies. Burnished by the intense friction generated when entering the earth's atmosphere, the object had attained an odd, translucent hue. Riding warm air currents and hiding itself by reflecting and refracting the day's intense sunshine, the craft appeared almost translucent. Had anyone seen it, they would have dismissed it as a mirage, a freak shimmering of a heat haze in a place it oughtn't to be, a trick of the light and water vapour as the encroaching humidity of a midnight thunderstorm nudged up alongside the dregs of the afternoon's sweltering heatwave.

Ensconced in the boughs of a tree in Brockwell Park, the ship was afforded some protection against prying eyes. Even if anyone had been looking in the right place this June 1998 afternoon, they'd have dismissed the trickles of green oleaginous liquid winding their way down the cracks of the tree trunk's bark as some sort of sap that had risen in tandem with the temperature. The couple who would soon emerge from beneath the tree looked, to all intents and purposes, like normal human beings in their early twenties. The intense green of their eyes may have provoked a momentary double-take from anyone who'd got close enough, but they remained undisturbed as they crossed the park and headed for the centre of Brixton.

Yet if any of the denizens of Effra Road had known what evil walked among them; had the young men playing pool in the George Canning pub understood the threat posed by the tall bleached blonde man and his Asiatic female companion to the very fabric of human civilisation; should someone parking their car on the forecourt of the Halfords superstore stopped dead in their tracks and broken into a cold sweat with the dread of their appearance - well, they wouldn't have been able

9

to do much about it anyway. The visitors had travelled inconceivable distances from their dying home world to survey the quality of the planet's crop, and someone detecting them or realising the diabolical purpose of their mission would have been dealt with swiftly, noiselessly and completely. Their reconnaissance was far too important for them to take any chances.

And so the strangers passed unnoticed along Brixton High Road, indistinguishable from the knots of people clustered around the tables outside the Fridge Bar, unmolested by the vagrant cadging small change by the Barclays cash dispenser, until they disappeared into the flood of excitable folk pouring from the tube station towards Stockwell Road. Mixing with humans was easy: they'd spent their lives, all three hundred and seventy-plus earth years, preparing for this day. Their command of every known nuance of every language they were likely to encounter had been studied and digested. They were safe now. And they knew what they had to do.

The brains were what their people were after. Their mission was to assess the quality of the neural networks the planet had to offer. Time was running short; another two generations and their species would cease to exist unless suitable thought-patterns could be consumed and absorbed. There was urgency in their steps as they filed along with the crowd.

But their preparation had been flawed. Instead of pointing them to the seats of learning, the universities, libraries and garret rooms of cloistered academe, the aliens believed that the greatest minds would cause crowds to gather around them, that the density of cogitative matter would somehow induce less powerful intellects to spiral ever closer. Had they arrived at Wembley on Cup Final day they would have made the mistake of thinking that the referee was the most intelligent man on the planet. After all, they would reason, tens of thousands of people had gathered there just to be close to him. How wrong can you be?

For some reason they managed to bypass the security at the

Academy; they probably turned themselves invisible
or something. Anyway, once they were inside the cavernously
ceilinged and rather ornate room they began to push their way
to the front.

A roar alerted them to the beginning of the ceremony on the
stage. The thousands of people, clustered together to pay
homage to their intellectual leaders, were baying raucously.
The male alien grinned nervously at his companion. The time
was drawing close.

Several men in orange boiler suits took up their positions
across the stage. They looked like they'd arrived to fix
someone's guttering or offer to sell the throng a set of retreads,
but the aliens didn't know that. Television screens behind them
displayed ever-changing linear geometric figures while intense
beams of light dashed across the performance area. A husky
woodwind sound tumbled from the banks of loudspeakers at
either side of the stage and the sea of bodies the aliens were
a part of suddenly surged forward. The noise was deafening.
The moment was almost upon them.

Suddenly, there in the centre of the tableau, a glowing figure
appeared. Wearing a blue suit and cape which seemed to
radiate as the light beams struck it, the figure moved forward,
towards the sea, unknowingly about to seal the destiny of his
kind. The aliens' hearts would have been in their mouths, if
they'd had hearts. Or mouths.

This was it: the culmination of their searching, planning,
preparation and journeying. They would soon know whether
the human brain would provide them with the nourishment
they craved. The blue figure was about to speak: by his words
would they know him.

"I've got the brand new doo-doo guaranteed like yoo-hoo,"
Mike D - for it was he - began. "I'm on like Doctor John, yeah,
Mister Zu-Zu."

The female alien looked helplessly and incredulously into
the fierce green eyes of her companion. "Fuckin' 'ell!" she
wailed. "We're knackered!" And with that the creatures

disappeared in a puff of intense disappointment, never again to pass by this corner of the galaxy.

And to think - evil aliens would have eaten our brains with spoons if it hadn't been for them pesky Beastie Boys.

Well, it could happen. And even if it couldn't, it is this writer's contention that the Beastie Boys are probably the most important band in the world today. This book is my attempt to find out why.

What interests me about the Beasties should be abundantly clear in the text, but a couple of points should be clarified in advance. Firstly, were I not averse to being a tad pretentious, I might choose to describe myself as a student of hip-hop culture: as such I see the Beastie Boys primarily as a hip-hop group. I have therefore concentrated on this line of approach to the band as I feel that it is correct: moreover, as will become clear as the book's narrative progresses, the band's relationship with hip-hop culture has informed much of their music, attitudes and lifestyle, and hip-hop has changed too as a result of the Beasties and their involvement in it. The fact that they have been more successful in recent years with the college/alternative music crowd is not irrelevant, but it is, I believe, a function of their hip-hop heritage and is therefore best understood by examining the band's story from a hip-hop perspective. Secondly, as someone who watched the Beastie story develop from London, my personal perspective is formed from a British standpoint. I mention this here not as a warning or an apology, but merely as a clarification and a partial explanation.

The Beastie Boys have been, and continue to mean, many different things to many different people. This is partially what makes them so boundlessly fascinating, and is a key part of both their longevity and their importance. I hope you will recognise your own version of the Beastie Boys in these pages, but I also hope you'll have a clearer understanding of some of the other ones too.

CHAPTER ONE

"The Beasties got married for life when they were young adolescents and went through all these stages. Probably they always intended to be together. There are a lot of kids who make that kind of promise and then fall apart for any number of reasons, but these guys always had a vision of themselves being together as creative artists."
Bill Adler, hip-hop historian and former publicist for the Beastie Boys while they were signed to Def Jam.

Although these days they seem inseparable, the Beastie Boys started out life in different bands. Michael Diamond, born on November 20th, 1965 to art dealer parents, was originally a vocalist in a band called The Young Aborigines. His cohorts in this short-lived enterprise were guitarist John Berry and drummer Kate Shellenbach. To describe their career as short-lived would be putting it mildly: they called it a day after their second gig, which had taken place on the same day as their first.

These three formed the Beasties in New York in 1981 along with their friend Adam Yauch. The son of an architect, born 5th August 1964, Yauch started out as a bassist. Tellingly, he and Diamond had first met at a gig by the widely respected Washington DC black hardcore punk band Bad Brains when still in their early teens: it must have been coincidence, but it seems almost karmic that a white band who would make an indelible impression on the black music form, hip-hop, came together while watching a black band playing music that came from an almost totally white musical culture. Diamond recalled the meeting during a 1998 interview with *NME*'s Ted Kessler. "I was this incredibly awkward punk rock kid with spiky hair. I'd tried to dye it orange but it hadn't really worked at all, and it looked like shit. I was going to a lot of punk rock shows on my own because I didn't have any friends who were into that. And because I was young and he [Yauch] was young, a lot younger than most people at the gigs, we became part of this group of kids who went to clubs and to see bands together. I don't know if it's to do with being from New York or just from being insecure, but we certainly didn't just stroll up to each other and say 'What's up'. We scowled at each other for some time first."

Meanwhile, future Beastie Adam Horovitz, the son of playwright Israel, was thrashing about in a hardcore band called The Young And The Useless. Suitably for one who would be accused of terrorising society, he was born, in 1966, on Halloween. He wouldn't meet his latterday band mates until a while later, again at a gig, though - again, tellingly - it wasn't a punk event. It was at a rap show by the Sugarhill Records-signed Funky Four Plus One More, a later line-up of a band whose classic 'It's The Joint' would be referenced and sampled by the Beasties several times in the ensuing years.

The Beastie Boys and The Young And The Useless played gigs around Manhattan's punk cellars during the first eighteen months of the 1980s. Venues such as A7, CBGB's and Max's Kansas City provided them with their first footings in live performance, although the pre-Horovitz line-up's first ever gig was at Adam Yauch's seventeenth birthday party, held in John's loft. Kate Schellenbach's recollections a few years later give a fair indication of where the early Beasties' heads were at: "They were just the same as they are now," she maintained in the 1989 press biography released prior to their second album. "Loud, obnoxious and ugly, and a lot of fun rather than a serious hardcore band. Whereas other bands, just as awful as the Beastie Boys, would actually believe they were good, for Mike and Adam the whole point was to be terrible and to admit it."

The soon-to-be trio had wanted to be rock stars since their pre-teen years. Adam Yauch later told *Guitar World* that "I always wanted a bass when I was a kid, though I didn't get one at first. My parents were too tired of buying me things that would just end up in the closet. I knew this girl who had a bass, and I'd go over to her house to play. My parents eventually rented one for me on the condition that if I played it, I could have it." In the same magazine, Horovitz remembered his first electric guitar, and why he wanted one: "For my twelfth birthday my Mom and all her friends got me a guitar and a little practice amp. I talked about playing guitar all the time - I was listening to a lot of Kiss, and I wanted to be Ace. I thought 'Shock Me' - the song where Ace sings - was the shit! 'Making Love' too. So my Mom and her friends bought me a Hondo II Professional."

Like so many young men of their generation, the nascent Beasties had been attracted to punk by the music's energy and its anti-establishment stance. But punk rock in the early '80s in New York was a very different creature to that which had crawled out of London almost a decade earlier. The Big Apple was home to the New York Dolls (managed by Malcolm McLaren, the svengali figure behind the Sex Pistols, who would jump on the hip-hop bandwagon around the same time as the Beasties in the mid-80s) and Johnny Thunders, artists who became massive influences on the first wave of British punk. The city also produced the goofier but very much punk-inspired Ramones, but despite these legacies, New York didn't experience an explosion of this music in the same way British cities like London or Manchester did. By the early '80s America seemed to be crying out for its own punk-like catharsis, and one of the ways this need manifested itself was in the growth of a post-punk hardcore scene. Though more readily associated with Washington DC than New York, American hardcore is to this day synonymous with an uncompromising seriousness of purpose. Many hardcore bands are "straight edge", meaning they eschew drinking or drug use, and the majority of the music is concerned with socio-political point-making. At its best, hardcore can transcend such constraints and produce music that succeeds despite (or perhaps because of) the limitations of the form: Washington band Fugazi have become the scene's *de facto* leaders, although they, being opposed to all forms of authoritarianism and social inequality, don't see it that way, and their determination to remain outside the music business is reflected in their edgy, dramatic and compelling records just as much as in the uncompromising attitude they take in manufacturing, distributing and selling them. At the other end of the spectrum, though, hardcore can be pretty grim stuff.

This clearly seems to have been the Beastie Boys' impression when they began their irreverent stab at being a hardcore band. Exhibiting, even at such an early stage, the self-deprecating humour that would become a defining trait of their music over the coming years, the band tried to introduce a few laughs to the po-faced hardcore scene. They were not particularly successful.

It's safe to say the Beastie Boys, even before Horovitz joined, didn't behave exactly in keeping with the inordinately serious vibe of the hardcore scene, and their evident glee in attempting to add a lighter shade to the music's palette divided opinion on them. Some influential figures were clearly impressed: HR of Bad Brains caught a Beastie show and asked them to support his group at Max's Kansas City, while other people, such as Phoebe and Simon Stringer of North Carolina, clearly disagreed. "The Beastie Boys are the most feeble band I have ever and will ever seen or see," the couple wrote, somewhat confusingly, in a letter to the band, later reprinted in the sleeve notes to *Some Old Bullshit*: "Please save face and bow out of this mess as gracefully as you can before everyone realises the same thing that we did." (Little did the correspondents know back then, but the Beastie Boys had already split up on several occasions. By the time they got to record their debut release they'd already called it a day, splitting after the Bad Brains support because, as Diamond put it in the *Some Old Bullshit* sleeve, "it didn't seem funny anymore". They split again before the record's eventual release convinced them to "re-form" for some gigs.)

One of the band's mates, Dave Parsons, ran a record shop called Rat Cage that the group and their friends frequented at the time. "We came across Johnny Thunders selling autographed 10" x 8" glossies outside Rat Cage to feed his heroin habit," Adrock told Stuart Clark at *Hot Press* in 1994. "Stiv [Bators], Johnny and most of the other Dolls are dead by now which, I think, underlines the redundancy of the era." Parsons had decided to start a label named after his shop, and, much to the Horovitz-less Beasties' delight, he asked them to make a record for this new imprint. The 'Polly Wog Stew' EP was recorded in a single winter weekend late in 1981 in a studio in the same building as Parsons' shop. The boss of the fledgling label had access to the studio for free because it was then on the verge of being shut down. Although the band didn't have time to mix the record before the studio was closed, the 7" EP was nevertheless released by Parsons early in 1982.

An amateurish slew of fuzztone guitars, bluebottle bass and shouting, 'Polly Wog Stew' is not the finest recorded work the Beasties ever produced. Its eight tracks, though, do reveal something of the group's later pre-occupations and hint at why their time in the hardcore wilderness was not idly spent. All hardcore bands were seemingly obliged to have at least one anti-police song, and in 'Transit Cop' the Beasties vent their spleen at traffic police: the technique they would employ most fruitfully on their debut LP *Licensed To Ill* - blowing trivial problems up to a level their more serious-minded musical peers would use to talk about *real* issues - is here given an early try-out. 'Michelle's Farm' finds them insulting one another; again, a recurring theme in their later work ("you're so ugly, Adam, you look like a pig farmer"), and displays hints of the wordplay that would soon develop. 'Egg Raid On Mojo' was revisited in infinitely more engaging form on the *Paul's Boutique* album, where elements of it were overhauled to make the track 'Egg Man', while the eponymous 'Beastie Boys' spells out the band's name and does little else. Diamond has frequently maintained that the moniker is an acronym, standing for Boys Entering Anarchistic States Towards Internal Excellence. Hip-hop music doesn't have a monopoly on this trend, but the genre certainly has more than its fair share of such appellations: e.g. KRS-ONE (Knowledge Reigns Supreme Over Nearly Everyone), Blade (Beneficial Living Always Develops through Experience) and the Wu-Tang Clan track 'C.R.E.A.M.' ('Cash Rules Everything Around Me'). As the band were still part of the hardcore genre when they settled on the name, and given (a) that 'Beastie Boys' doesn't include the words, just the initial letters, and (b) the whole phrase is more than a little cumbersome, it seems safe to assume the "meaning" to the name was concocted after the band had already begun using it.

John Berry's departure cleared the way for the Beasties to take more recognisable shape (Berry went on to join Thwig). He jumped ship shortly after the EP's release and the subsequent gigs, and, in looking around for a replacement, Yauch, Diamond and Schellenbach settled quickly on Horovitz. The Young And The Useless had opened gigs for the Beasties on several occasions, and not only did Adam's guitar style seem suitably rudimentary, his band had even covered some Beastie Boys songs, so he didn't require much tutelage. Tragically for the history of western music, this move spelled the end for The Young And The Useless. "We fell apart really bad," Horovitz told *Guitar World*. "The drummer went to military school in New Jersey."

Yet even as this new line-up was settling in, the Beasties' listening habits were changing. Leaning increasingly towards the new sounds emanating from New York's black neighbourhoods, the Beasties spent 1982 and 1983 devouring hip-hop.

This was the era when the still relatively new music began to spread outside the communities that had spawned it, and plenty of curious onlookers got caught up in the excitement.

The Clash invited the epochal rap group Grandmaster Flash and the Furious Five to support them at a sold-out New York residency, Blondie released the rap-inflected love song to the hip-hop movement, 'Rapture', and the music's visual equivalent - graffiti art - began to get shown in downtown galleries as street-spawned artists like Jean-Michel Basquiat began to get taken seriously by the notoriously stuffy NY art establishment. Breakdancers began to throw down at Manhattan niteries like the Mudd Club, influential hip-hop DJs such as Afrika Bambaataa and Flash got booked to play in the more eclectic and progressive downtown clubs, and the whole movement was embraced by the open-minded but predominantly white and affluent Greenwich Village crowd.

Hip-hop became, for those that wanted it, New York's punk rock. Dynamic, exciting, opinionated and provocative, the new music-based culture galvanised people and quickly became compulsive. To a band like the Beasties it must have been a godsend: after underground America had spent years struggling to recreate the aura of punk, here at last was the home-grown real thing - a revolutionary music set to blow everything before it out of the water, cheap and easy to make, enabling its practitioners to find their own sound, style and voice. "Attitude-wise, hardcore and rap are remarkably similar," Diamond told American-based British hip-hop journalist Frank Owen, writing in *Newsday* in 1992. "The energy is the same. And you can express yourself without having had to study music for fifteen years. I used to say that the only difference was that with punk rock you have funny haircuts, whereas with rap you have funny hats."

The Beasties first heard rap on the subway trains as they rode to and from Yauch's place in Brooklyn to Manhattan and back - bootlegged cassettes of rap battles from Harlem and the Bronx, tapes of early singles on the Enjoy and Sugarhill labels, played on the tape machines of young black kids from Uptown, Brooklyn and Queens. "The first hip-hop I ever heard - really before it was ever on wax - was on the subway when

I was going to school hearing kids playing battle tapes," Mike D told Jim Treymayne of *DJ Times* in 1994. "As soon as [Sugarhill Gang's] 'Rapper's Delight' or 'Flash To The Beat' by Grandmaster Flash came out, we'd start to request them downtown. A DJ who was influential - and this wasn't a hip-hop thing - was this woman Anita Sarko who used to play clubs like Mudd Club. We'd convince her to play stuff. She played No Wave stuff, but also New Wave dance stuff. She was the first downtown DJ we could convince to play 'Birthday Party Rap' or 'Spoonin' Rap'. Another influential DJ was [Afrika] Bambaataa and that definitely changed the world for us when we heard him spin. First of all, he had this presence - not as a performer or someone on-stage - but when he came into the place, him and his whole Zulu Nation crew, it was this presence. He just took over the vibe, dominated the vibe, he *made* the vibe. The thing that really fucked us up was that we expected him to play hip-hop jams, and he did, but the whole shit was mixing in 'Apache' or 'Son Of Scorpio' and then he'd go into the craziest pop record and make it work, like "Oh Mikki, you're so fine!" That's what I mean by freakin' it. Bam could mix the most unlikely records and make it work."

Mike would later pay a tribute to this period of learning on the band's fourth LP, *Ill Communication*. On the song 'Root Down', he paints a vivid verbal picture of those early morning journeys to school that would ultimately be of more use to his career than what he learned in class. Recalling his train journey to High Street station, still frantically scribbling his homework, the teenager recalled listening to tapes of legendary emcee battles, "like Harlem World battles on the Zulu Beat show/It's Kool Moe Dee vs Busy Bee - there's one you should know."

Exposed to hip-hop's visceral thrills and becoming absorbed by the cultural explosion happening around them, it could only be a matter of time before the Beasties made their tentative first steps into rap music. And, as tentative first steps go, 'Cookie Puss' found them playing the enthusiastic toddler to perfection: struggling to stand up but shouting so loud they still managed to attract plenty of attention.

'Cookie Puss' doesn't have any lyrics, so to speak, but against its quite stark, hip-hop influenced beats, it sets samples from a prank telephone call the band made to an ice cream parlour. The Carvel ice cream company made a type of ice cream cake called a Cookie Puss, and the band had taped a phone call to their local store wherein they ask to speak to Cookie Puss as though it was a person. They then abuse the hapless telephonist when she, inevitably, fails to comply with their request. In its juvenile content and brattish, sexist tone, 'Cookie Puss' is a clear indication of where the Beasties were heading thematically. It is not, however, a particularly good record, and its odd, reggae-tinged B-side, 'Beastie Revolution', is little better. Released as a 12" (indicative of the fact that rap 12" singles were now more representative of what the band were listening to than the hardcore 7"s of yore) on Rat Cage in the second half of 1983, the record would nevertheless prove to be of pivotal importance to the band's immediate future prospects: improbably, it brought them both important hook-ups and a huge wad of cash.

The latter arrived after friends alerted the band to the fact that, bizarrely, 'Beastie Revolution' had allegedly been sampled by no less prestigious a corporation than British Airways for one of their TV advertisements. Quite how BA or, more pertinently, their advertising agency, came to be listening to a fairly awful approximation of reggae from a bunch of New York goofballs found only on the B-side of a novelty rap record about an ice cream cake will probably remain unclear for the rest of time.

Though one of the most widely-reported stories about the Beasties' early years, quoted in a 1987 *Spin* magazine feature and repeated as gospel thereafter, the BA farrago exhibits the classic elements of a band-created wind-up: the Beastie Boys respond to a dis from a world famous brand name and come out of it with an improbably large sum of money. It's like something out of one of their lyrics, and it's certainly no more believable than their stories about forming bands with uber-geek comic actor Rick Moranis or recording albums in submarines. BA have no record of such a lawsuit, though conspiracy theorists would surely contend that "they would say that, wouldn't they?"

This, though, is the story the Beasties have stuck to ever since. So, as they tell it, one lawsuit later, they allegedly found themselves better off to the tune of $40,000, enabling them to move out of their parents' homes and into a decrepit Chinatown loft. Though it had some advantages, salubrious accommodation it was not.

"It was called a loft, but it was really a small apartment," the band told *Spin*'s Tom Cushman. "The ceiling was about seven feet high. The floorboards from the sweatshop above us were our ceiling. And they'd start early in the morning, about seven o'clock. It was the only thing we could afford; but aside from that, we could play music at any time of night, as loud as we could possibly get our amps. We'd come home at four in the morning, drunk, and play music. [Rent] was $500. We moved there when we got the British Airways money and we rebuilt the whole thing. The floor was made of blacktop. It was once wood, but someone had poured tar over it. There were so many rats we bought pellet guns. In the basement was a trendy Korean whorehouse, called Club 59. Silver door, completely tacky. None of the women were at all pretty. They were all around 35 or 37 and they'd been around the block too many times."

The rodent problem was one the Beasties had a simple and effective solution to. During an interview with *NME*'s Steven Wells one unfortunate creature made the mistake of venturing into view. The group shot, stamped and eventually bludgeoned the thing to death with a baseball bat. The close proximity of the brothel, though, posed different complications, as the band told their friend and co-conspirator Bob Mack in *Dirt* magazine some years later. At the end of their first month in their new pad, the group were somewhat surprised to be presented with an electricity bill for $800. "We go to the landlord," Yauch remembered, "and ask him what's up with it. [He] calls Peter the Pimp, for real. So Peter comes upstairs, he's like Vietnamese I think, this dude comes up with shorts on and like those sunglasses, looks like something right out of one of those movies, and his hair like all kind of back, and he just comes in and says 'Come with me'. And we go and we didn't know what the fuck was going on so we go and get on the elevator. He takes us next door, into the whorehouse, and he explained to us that he had tapped into our power because he wasn't a legal resident of the United States so he needed to get electricity, and then he just sat us down in the room with all of the uh…women, and he walked out of the room and just left us there, and they were like offering us fruit and drinks and stuff like that, and we were like, 'Ah, no thanks.' When he finally realised that we weren't going for it he came back and called us into the other room and just whipped a stack of money out of his pocket and peeled off eight hundred bucks and paid our whole bill."

At this point the video director Spike Jonze, who's been sitting in on the interview, makes a suggestion. "You were dealing electricity," he claims. "You could say," agrees a thoughtful Yauch.

Aside from the cash and the freedom it provided - not to mention the opportunity the band got to become New York's smallest power supply company - 'Cookie Puss' got people talking. "There was *always* a buzz about the Beasties," Bill Adler, the band's press officer during their time with Def Jam, maintains. And it was 'Cookie Puss' that started that buzz. The record got the Beasties noticed by New York's hip-hop community.

Fab 5 Freddy was a graffiti artist who played a pivotal role in introducing artists to rappers and dancers and helping to form the whole culture of hip-hop. He would later go on to run record labels and find international fame and recognition as a VJ on *Yo! MTV Raps*, the cable video station's only specialist hip-hop show. During the mid '80s Freddy was a luminary on the nascent graffiti/gallery scene; he had introduced post-punk power pop band Blondie to hip-hop culture, and he is namechecked during their 'Rapture' single. "They became the perfect incarnation or combination of the two aesthetics," he says today, reminiscing about the Beasties' melding of punk and rap musics and sensibilities prior to the middle of the decade. "Them guys were good buddies, they were boppin' around the scene at that time. I was showin' at the galleries and they would come in and stand around real quiet. They were cool, but I didn't know who they was until I heard a record called 'Cookie Puss'. I was like, 'That is fuckin' genius! Who are these guys?' The next thing you know Russell snatched 'em, Rick got involved… and the rest was history."

Russell Simmons and Rick Rubin would become the two most influential figures outside of the band for the next four years of the Beastie Boys story. The duo had met at a New York club, Danceteria, and couldn't have made on odder pairing. Yet Rubin, the white, long-haired heavy rock fan and film student, and Simmons, the style-conscious black entrepreneur with a burgeoning career in rap music that dated back to before the first hip-hop records had been made, had much more in common than appearances would have suggested. "Russell liked beat-oriented material derived from R&B, like Al Green and James Brown, and I liked beat-oriented material based in rock, like AC/DC and Aerosmith," Rubin said of their compatibility in the sleevenotes to the Def Jam compilation album, *Kick It!* "In both cases, it was dance music that was a reaction against boring disco."
    "If the white kids had liked hardcore, I would never have gotten involved in rap music," Rubin continued, explaining how a fan of hardcore punk bands like Black Flag and Minor Threat ended up producing a string of classic rap releases, and into the bargain illustrating the ties that would bind him for

a few years to the similarly inclined Beastie Boys. "The fact that new music is stifled, instead of embraced, by white teens, is what forced me to like rap music. The white kids in my school liked the Stones, Sabbath, The Who or Zeppelin, groups that were either dead or might as well have been. The black kids in my school were always waiting for the new rap record to come out. There was a scene building in rap, but not in hardcore."

The Beasties were realising the same thing. "We got tired of the hardcore scene. It was very negative," Mike D told *Rock And Soul*'s Scott Mehno in 1987. "The rap scene is a lot better because the rappers all have more camaraderie with each other." This, coupled with the desire to capitalise on 'Cookie Puss's notoriety and play this and material like it live, was what galvanised them initially towards playing hip-hop in preference to hardcore. "We were getting a black audience through that song, but we couldn't play 'Cookie Puss' live; the only thing we could do like it was rapping," Diamond explained to *Detroit Free Press* journalist Gary Graff in 1987. But meeting Rick provided the turning point. "Rick became our manager and DJ," Diamond told Scott Mehno. "Then we met Russell Simmons and he took us all under his wing. People still hated us, but we liked what we were doing."

"We needed a DJ and Rick was the only guy we knew with all the equipment," Diamond recounted to *Hot Press* in 1994, "including, for some reason, a bubble machine which was straight out of *Saturday Night Fever*." Kate Schellenbach, who would later claim that Rubin had encouraged the three to behave in a sexist manner, took her leave. The band effected a seamless transition, and gave themselves the hip-hop derived names they still use today - Michael Diamond becoming Mike D, emcee Adam Yauch abbreviating his title to MCA and Adam Horovitz took up the mantle of The King Adrock - and started to make serious moves into this dazzling new musical world.

With Rubin on the wheels of steel, adopting the suitable

sobriquet DJ Double R, the Beasties were free at last to abandon their instruments and concentrate on rapping. And with Russell's help they began to move from playing mainly white hardcore punk gigs to predominantly black rap events. "We opened for Kurtis Blow and UTFO at this hardcore black disco club called the Encore Club," Mike told *Details'* Pat Blashill in 1994. "We had to talk our way inside, the club was so full. The place smelled like a cross between mentholated cigarettes and angel dust. We go on and people looked at us like we were out of our minds. We were honestly, genuinely *alien*, in the truest sense." Adrock recalled probably the same gig as an altogether more scary proposition. "I remember one night doing a gig in a real rough part of town with Kurtis Blow and it was touch and go whether we were going to get out alive," he told journalist Stuart Clark in 1994. "We [got] stared at like we were from outer space, which was a little disconcerting. In that kind of situation, you have to be good at what you do or you're dead."

Simmons and Rubin had been plotting something for months, and 1984 saw the launch of a new joint venture, the Def Jam record label. From modest beginnings - the office was in Rick's New York University student accommodation - Def Jam would grow to become arguably the most influential record label in the world during the latter part of the '80s. Acolytes of both Simmons and Rubin from before the label got launched, it was inevitable that the Beastie Boys would make rap records on it. Initially, though, the group's role was almost as unpaid A&R men. "We helped 'em discover people like LL Cool J and Public Enemy who had their shit together but couldn't get a deal," Mike told Clark. "In the early days it was family." It is an interesting aside to note, however, that although Cool J acknowledges a debt to the Beasties for discovering him, Public Enemy's Chuck D, in his book *Fight The Power - Rap, Race and Reality doe*sn't mention their input, saying only that Rubin had been keen to sign his group for some time before it actually happened. Prior to signing to Def

Jam, Public Enemy had released a single under the name Spectrum City, and it is entirely conceivable that one or more of the Beasties could have drawn this record to Rubin's attention.

Whatever the truth about these issues, the irrefutable fact remains that the first Def Jam single - LL Cool J's 'I Need A Beat' - was released in October '84. In his entertaining autobiography, *I Make My Own Rules*, Cool J remembers how much he owes to the Beasties, and to Horovitz in particular. He had sent a demo tape to Rubin at the address he'd put on the first single he'd made, T La Rock's 'It's Yours', and had been calling the producer almost daily but Rick hadn't come across the tape. Suddenly, though, Rubin called the teenage rapper back, said he'd got the tape and wanted to arrange a meeting. LL visited Rubin in his NYU dormitory room. "I had been speaking to Rick for weeks and could have sworn he was a black man," Cool J writes. "But there he was, a white Jewish guy. This was a rap producer? Hell, no. I had always thought rap music was produced by blacks. It was our music, our vibe. But obviously I was wrong and I shrugged it off. Hey, I didn't care if Rick Rubin was purple and worshipped penguins. He could have been Ronald McDonald, as long as I got a record deal. He laughed at my reaction to him and invited me up to the tiny room at the end of the hall. Mattresses were on the floor and records and tapes were thrown everywhere. I could see how my tape would have gotten lost. In fact, if it wasn't for Adrock of the Beastie Boys, I might still be sending in those tapes. Adrock had been chillin' in Rick's room, rummaging through all the tapes, and somehow he fished mine out and played it. I guess he liked what he heard and brought it to Rick's attention. My man Adrock: Good lookin' out, baby!"

But merely alerting the new company to other talent wasn't ever going to be the Beastie Boys role, and they would soon release their own first rap record proper. Fittingly, perhaps, 'Rock Hard/Beastie Groove' followed hot on LL's heels and became the second Def Jam release in November 1984. Yet anyone picking it up having first heard 'Cookie Puss' would have been hard pressed to recognise the same band at work: the transformation the group made during 1984 is astonishing by anyone's standards. Although Mike now describes 'Rock Hard' as "pretty embarrassing", the track - which sampled AC/DC's 'Back In Black' nearly three years before Boogie Down Productions tried the same trick - alerted those who heard it to rappers with genuine talent and singular vision, one that transcended racial barriers to hit hard with fans of the new music. Even their rivals couldn't fail to be impressed.

"The record was incredible," remembers Joseph 'Run' Simmons. Alongside Darrel [DMC] McDaniels and DJ Jam Master Jay, aka Jason Mizzell, Run was part of the hugely respected and influential group Run DMC. Joseph was Russell Simmons' brother, and his band, managed by Russell through his Rushtown Management company, had by the end of 1984 already released an eponymous album on the Profile label that contained the epochal track 'Rock Box', probably the earliest incorporation of rap with rock guitars. Because of this, as well as their management and the involvement of Rubin on their 1986 LP, *Raising Hell*, Run DMC are often thought of as a Def Jam band, though in reality they never recorded for the label. They were definitely part of the extended family, though, and Run's first impressions of the Beasties - based around their talent as rappers rather than their race or colour - were formed after coming into contact with them through his brother and Rubin. "They was young white b-boys with musical talent, and I believed in their first rap record that I heard ['Rock Hard']. I loved that."

Though 'Rock Hard' is rudimentary, it could easily have found a place on the band's debut album - it's similar in shade and tone and uses rock samples and atmospherics to scintillating effect. Lyrically it has little that was new to offer, which is probably why Diamond doesn't seem to rate it nowadays, but there are clues as to how the band viewed themselves that seem pertinent to any discussion of the way they blended genres and attitudes to create their new aesthetic. "I can play the drums," shouts Diamond; "I can play guitar," Adrock, erm, ads; "Not just b-boys but real rock stars" - an inversion of the actual story, perhaps, but as a joyous thrash attempting to legitimise rap in the face of music business traditionalism it works brilliantly. It's also been a very influential record. 'Rock Hard' pre-dated every rock/rap fusion other than Run DMC's 'Rock Box' from the previous year. Lyrically, the Beasties single may be juvenile, but it's every bit as intricate as anything anyone else was doing (even a year later, Run DMC's 'King Of Rock' would sport decidedly post-Beastie style lyrics like "When we play jams we break two needles/There's three of us but we're not The Beatles"). There was a precedent for 'Rock Hard's sound, but the Beasties weren't bothered. Their pride in being Beasties was already evident. "We're here, we're now, and the battle's won," they boasted, gloriously.

Even better was the B-side, 'Beastie Groove'. Set against a pacy but minimal drum program that keeps speeding up and slowing down throughout, the three emcees show just how skilled they had become in such a short period of time. Chorusing and interrupting each other in a style that would typify many of their best records, Mike D, Adrock and MCA each get extended chances to shine. And while the subject matter is the same childish and sex-obsessed splather as can be found on their debut album, there are few better examples of their skill as rappers to be found anywhere in their oeuvre. In between implausible boasts about being "on the mic in Rome and Capri" and Adrock's hysterical couplet "I'm a man who needs no introduction/Got a big tool of reproduction," there's some incredible writing and dexterous vocalising. Even Rick Rubin's somewhat rustic attempts at scratching seem to work, and it's interesting to note that the overall sound of the instrumental portions of the track isn't too far away from the highly revered and seriously acclaimed Boogie Down

Productions LP, 'Criminal Minded', which wouldn't be released until 1987. Substantively, perhaps, this is a slight record, but stylistically it's a revelation.

Def Jam also released a Beastie-related single early the following year. 'Drum Machine', Def Jam's fourth 12", was the work of MCA and Burzootie, aka Jay Burnett, a putative programmer and engineer who'd worked with the group on the 'Rock Hard' record. "It was a remake of something Burnett had made on his own, earlier, like crap metal/electronica/rap synthesis," remembers Bill Adler, "and when MCA got in with him for Def Jam it was much more rock rap, a Beasties record."

To many rap purists, MCA has always seemed to have the best rap voice, and it made a certain amount of sense to give him an entire single to himself. And 'Drum Machine' is a decent enough record, but it doesn't stand out from the crowd. Musically it rehashes a few electro moves and fits nicely into the mechanised style of rap that was then on the wane. But vocally, which should have been the single's strongest suit, you keep missing Diamond and Horovitz. "Russ didn't disparage MCA," Adler notes, "he said MCA has good conventional skill whereas Adrock and MCA don't sound like anyone else and that's what cool about them." And it's this individuality that 'Drum Machine' lacks. Even at this early stage the Beastie Boys had developed a chemistry between the three voices that made almost everything else seem somehow less exciting. MCA's record merely served to underline this, and should have warned the label off further experimentation in a similar direction (the band themselves took heed, and even in a career as distinguished by doing whatever felt right, more than a decade would elapse before Yauch recorded another solo rap vocal track).

Otherwise it was a case of onwards and upwards for the band, with the occasional bit of sideways motion thrown in at Simmons' behest. When representatives of Madonna called him to try to book comedic overweight rap trio The Fat Boys for her forthcoming US tour, Simmons thought on his feet. He wasn't going to let them know he didn't represent The Fat Boys. Run DMC weren't available, but Russ had the next best thing. Which is how the Beastie Boys ended up on the *Like A Virgin* tour.

"I don't know what that did for them, necessarily," is Adler's professional opinion of the exercise. "I guess it got them a lot of press and notoriety." The tour probably also helped solidify any cracks that might have threatened to appear in the trio's relationship with each other, as they braved baying crowds of pre-teens and their parents who seemed to not much enjoy their show. "It was thousands of screaming girls telling us to get lost," was Mike's impression of the tour. "We got a response from everybody," Horovitz told reporter Gary Graff two years later. "They liked us or hated us, but we never had a dull night." This tour afforded the band their first opportunity of playing at the huge and prestigious Madison Square Garden in New York. The night would live long in Beastie lore. Bill Adler told *The Los Angeles Times* "it was one of the classic mis-matches of all-time. They came on-stage in front of 20,000 screaming fifteen year old Madonna wannabes who'd never heard of them and they started saying things like, 'Don't you love us?' The booing was deafening...so MCA jumped on top of one of the speakers, grabbed his crotch and started insulting the audience in very graphic language. It was one of the great punk moments. I expected lightning to come down and strike him dead." One journal, evidently unimpressed with the Beasties' show, described the band as "a pimple on the face of the music industry." Madonna was advised to remove them from the bill, but chose not to. "They were going to throw us off the tour after the first few nights, but then our manager went and pleaded with Madonna in her dressing room and she decided not to kick us off," Yauch explained to writer Billy Miller. Some versions of the story suggest that Madonna watched their show one night in disguise as a member of the audience, and ended up insisting more vehemently that the Beasties remain on the road with her.

But all was far from lost. The Madonna tour made a decent talking point in interviews for years to come. The Beasties once claimed to have drilled a peep hole to spy on the iconic megastar, but came clean a few years later. "Drilling a hole through a hotel room roof?" asked a cagey Diamond when *NME*'s James Brown queried the story in 1992. "Well, actually we stole that from The Who, but it sounded good and I'm pretty sure it's been repeated often enough to have become true. It is true she took a shining to Yauch."

"People do not give Madonna the credit she deserves, man, she's a real outrageous fun-loving girl," he told British metal magazine *Kerrang!*. "That woman's wild, I swear on my life," added MCA. "She smashed a TV set on the *Virgin* tour one night, no shit, and she smashed it with a sledgehammer from the top, the manly way."

It was following the tour the band made their debut album. As a number of tracks, including 'Hold It Now, Hit It', 'Paul Revere' and 'Slow And Low', had already been recorded and released as singles or B-sides, the recording process was piecemeal. Going into studios late at night suited both the band, who wanted to party, and their label, who could avoid having to pay the much higher daytime hire rates. "The whole process of making that record was probably some of the best times we had," Mike would later maintain in *Hip Hop Connection*. "Going out to clubs and then in to the studio at two in the morning, hanging out with Rick." What they were like the rest of the time, when they weren't the Beastie Boys, is difficult to divine. Bill Adler remembers them as being very different in private.

"They were young and snotty - they were the Beastie Boys! They obviously would kinda put it on and become more 'beastly' in public. But there was definitely a little bit of an edge with them."

Adler had, at this point, already found himself in close daily contact with some of the biggest names in rap, an incredibly egotistical genre. Yet he found the Beasties to be something else again. "I'd worked with Kurtis Blow, Whodini, I'd worked with Run DMC, they were all managed by Russ too, Jekyll and Hyde...and they were all easier to get along with than the Beasties. The Beasties had that edge and Yauch in particular had an edge, a punk attitude. Yauch was a very angry guy - there was just a kind of a sullenness off of him. Mike D could be snotty. I think of all of them, I got along with Horovitz the best. But they were all very cool."

"There was a very sweet period in '84, '85 when Russ would throw these parties and the entire Rush/Def Jam posse would be in the house - Run DMC, Whodini and Kurtis Blow, Beastie Boys, LL would all show up, it was just fun, loose, and when they could relax and didn't have to be the Beasties they could be charming, they could be warm."

The public, though, wouldn't get to see that side of the Beastie Boys for years, and even then, only rarely. The next two years would be filled with spilled beer, baseball bats, swearing and shagging, but before all of that, the Beastie Boys had a music to define.

CHAPTER TWO

"When that record [Licensed To Ill] *came out and went to Number
One, it scared all of us. We were like, 'Is something wrong?
What the fuck's going on?'"*
Fab 5 Freddy

The Beasties had reached debut album time with no real
difficulty, and no significant mistakes had been made that
might cloud the immediate future. What was important now
was that their first long player was the equal of the best rap
albums already made, and that it continued to show that the
band were moving forward artistically and conceptually. That
Licensed To Ill did all this and more was a significant part of
why it was to become the fastest selling debut in the history of
one of the music industry's superpower labels, and why it
would remain the best-selling rap album for years to come.

Licensed To Ill arrived at a time just before hip-hop's first
expressionistic flowering: before a Queen's, New York, DJ
named Eric B brought a young rapper called Rakim into the
game and elevated the role of the emcee and the techniques of
sampling to the level of high art; before a homeless shelter
worker trading under the name of DJ Scott La Rock hooked up
with one of his clients, an ego on legs with a philosophical
mindset and a mission to change the world called KRS-ONE,
and made an album - *Criminal Minded* - that put the onus on
reality rhymes, precipitated gangsta rap and changed the
music for good; and before Long Island radio host Chuck D
honed his militant agenda into a band that would eventually
rival The Clash as perhaps the greatest rebel rock group of all
time, Public Enemy. But back in '86 the choice was stark: you
had Run DMC's manic, shouted declamations, you had LL's
super-slick braggadocio, you had the disappearing legends of

rap's formative years failing to come to terms with the new era of record deals and recording studios. Admittedly, there was the odd emcee trying something ever so slightly different, but all were basically in the shadows of a handful of established names. And suddenly you had three nerdy white kids rapping like they had clothes pegs on their noses who, for some unaccountable reason, sounded like they'd been born to it ("Some voices got treble, some voices got bass" they note on 'The New Style': "We got the kinda voices that are in your face"). Listening to Mike D, Adrock and MCA flowing, you came to one inescapable conclusion: not only could they out-rap pretty much anyone else around at the time, but they were doing it in an individual style.

Licensed To Ill's sleeve attracted little comment on release, but the passage of time has elevated its single joke to the status of acute metaphor. The front cover shows the Beasties' diamond-shaped logo emblazoned on the tail fin of a chunky metallic jet plane, in the place one would expect to see an airline motif. In itself this is a clue to the record's contents, the notion that the band have not only their own plane, but their own *airline*, parodying rap's then still burgeoning concern with conspicuous consumption. It's only on turning the record over that you realise the plane has crash landed into a barren and precipitous cliff face. Tee, and, indeed, hee. If the record's gatefold sleeve is opened up and the image is looked at in its entirety, there's also an undeniably phallic aspect surely not accidentally implied. In there somewhere is an echo of Led Zeppelin and the semi-legendary private jet they used to tour the globe, the location of some of the more excessive stories of on-the-road carnage reported in Stephen Davis' *Hammer Of The Gods*. Although the connection may seem somewhat fortuitous, there's no getting away from the fact that, in many regards, *Licensed To Ill* is essentially a cross between the Sex Pistols' *Never Mind The Bollocks* and *Led Zeppelin II*, albeit a hybrid birthed in the fertile amniotic fluid of hip-hop culture.

Like that crash-landing jet plane, *Licensed To Ill* seemed to come out of nowhere. And, just like the parched red rock the plane is sticking out of, the world *Licensed To Ill* slammed into was one poorly prepared for its unique blend of rock excess, proto-laddish juvenilia, hip-hop attitude and nerdish self-parody. The album had few antecedents, but the ones that did exist were pretty close to home.

There are a few notable precedents to, and influences on, this album which deserve some discussion. Rick Rubin had, perhaps a little naively, turned on their head whatever rules the hip-hop genre had about how to make beats a matter of months earlier when he produced LL Cool J's debut LP, *Radio*. This album took the most minimal of drum loops, mashed them through a drum machine and let the teenage LL spin his cocksure lyrical spells over the top. Listening to *Radio* after exposure to *Licensed...* is instructive and enlightening: the same relentlessly, almost monotonously pared-down sound predominates, and both records are unafraid to dabble in rock atmospherics and sonics. The major difference lies in how metal guitars are used: *Licensed To Ill* includes tracks with guitar solos and, in 'Fight For Your Right', a song that sticks to a fundamentally straightforward rock format, while *Radio* is content to *hint* at metal - a powerchord here, a guitar stab there: the unmistakable clang of the centre of a ride cymbal set against loops that simultaneously *suggest* a live drummer but that are arranged in robotic patterns a drummer would have immeasurable difficulties with. *Radio* sounds both live and human yet simultaneously remote, mechanical, dehumanised: a fractured music for times steeped in uncertainties.

Radio is, in effect, the skeleton of a recognisable rock album, missing only the fleshing out of the song structures with familiar instrumentation. Yet, as close as it is to white metal music, *Radio* was acclaimed as a work of hip-hop (and therefore black music) genius. Hailed as an instant b-boy classic, the record helped both Rubin and the Beastie Boys by giving them a credible platform from which *Licensed To Ill* could be launched, enabling the group to hit both the rep-obsessed rap crowd and the rock traditionalists with their concerns about song structures. Whether the plan was concocted this way or not, the results were both phenomenally successful and indelibly influential.

The other crucial formative influence on the sound of the Beasties' debut was provided by Run DMC's 1986 masterpiece, *Raising Hell*. The credits proclaim a joint production by Russell Simmons and Rick Rubin, and while there is little evidence to counter this assertion, *Raising Hell* is clearly the missing link in the chain of musical evolution that connects *Radio* with *Licensed To Ill*. By 1986 Run DMC had become a massively respected and well-established hip-hop band. Their flirtations with rock were nothing new, as tracks on their previous *King Of Rock* album illustrate, and these came to the fore on *Raising Hell*, their third LP. There's an assumption that Rubin, the lank-haired white metal freak, was more of a driving force behind the Beastie Boys' melding of rock with rap than Simmons, but even the most cursory of examinations of Run DMC's career will show that the latter's agenda had always included expanding the parameters of hip-hop culture beyond the music's predominantly black urban roots.

Run DMC's most conspicuous success was their massive cover of 'Walk This Way', a track that featured Steve Tyler and Joe Perry from Aerosmith (who'd written the song originally) on the record and in the video. 'Walk This Way' proved to be an epochal release, and its success marked a truly groundbreaking moment in the history of rap. The first rap video to gain the crucial exposure afforded by MTV in the United States, 'Walk This Way' became a global hit and formed a pivotal point in the still unbroken relationship between hardcore rap and heavy metal.

Elsewhere on *Raising Hell*, though, Run DMC stuck largely to a more straightforward hip-hop blueprint. 'Peter Piper' utilised a popular party break beat from '70s veteran Bob James' 'Welcome To The Mardi Gras', chiming cowbells circulating back and forth across a bubbling rhythm track. Whenever there's a hip-hop DJ competing in one of the various battles for world supremacy, or simply keen to show his skills on the twin turntables, you'll still hear snatches of both '...Mardi Gras' *and* 'Peter Piper'. 'My Adidas' and 'You Be Illin'', both singles, illustrate the group's fondness for, and deft handling of, the most minimal of beats. The former, a paean to the band's favourite brand of sneaker (Adidas - and the fact that Run DMC wore them without laces - became such an identifiable part of the group's persona that the German athletics giant belatedly produced a Run DMC shoe a couple of years later), is a bouncier, more skittish variant on the ruthlessly sharp beats of *Radio*, and the drum programming bears more than a passing resemblance to a couple of tracks from *Licensed To Ill*. 'You Be Illin'', which performed a valuable duty for the Beasties by explaining to the world outside a few New York street corners the meaning of the word "ill" in its new hip-hop context (for example, Run and D maintain that if you order a Big Mac at a Kentucky Fried Chicken restaurant, "you be illin'"), adds a booming bassline to some razor-sharp drum snaps. The title track finds Rubin laying down a stereotypical rock guitar line, while the closer, 'Proud To Be Black', is self-explanatory. And, in an uncanny echo of the fondness late '90s producers such as Puff Daddy have exhibited for incorporating samples from '80s pop hits into the hip-hop of the day, 'It's Tricky' found Run and DMC trading rhymes over a rough-hewn rock-rap reconstruction of celebrated choreographer Toni Basil's novelty hit 'Oh, Mickey'.

Street credible, massively self-assured, unswervingly *du jour* and as hard as nails, *Raising Hell* was both crucial and fundamental in making hip-hop part of the musical mainstream.

It's unclear whether Rubin and Simmons saw it as such at the time, but *Licensed To Ill* was a huge gamble for Def Jam. By the time the Beasties' first LP was ready to go, Def Jam had hitched itself up to Columbia, then the largest record label in the world, who would be able to get the new label's records wider distribution and who could back Simmons' and Rubin's understanding of the market for the music they put out with substantial financial clout. Def Jam was one of the first underground labels that had emerged from the hip-hop scene to maximise their sales potential through major label distribution. And while a Cool J album had the credibility and the cachet with the core audience - urban black youth - that gave the label a firm foundation on which to build, *Licensed To Ill* was a whole other ball game.

The album is, for the most part, a wickedly funny pastiche of hip-hop culture. As with all the best parodies, the intention is to create a humour that draws in those who are being parodied as much as it seeks to pander to the preconceptions of outsiders predisposed to sneer. To the Beasties' inestimable credit, *Licensed To Ill* is a very *loving* fun-poking exercise, one that, were it to have appeared even five years later, would have been the subject of ridicule and scorn.

Musically, *Licensed To Ill* is basic. Like much of the hip-hop of the time, it relies on a selection of beats concocted on machines like the legendary SP-12, a drum machine that allows the programmer to construct original percussive patterns using sampled drum sounds. For instance, 'Rhymin & Stealin', the opening track, uses a mixture of deck techniques and drum machine programming to turn a sequence of sampled John Bonham drums into a slow, loping, lazy hip-hop rhythm. Still a relatively new tool in the mid-80s, the SP-12 was behind most of the major stylistic advances in hip-hop music prior to the advent of cheap samplers with long sample times (which, oddly, merely facilitated a return to the "live" sounds a DJ could create by mixing records on a pair of turntables), and its distinctive sound underpins much of the rest of the album.

For a record routinely dismissed as immature and embarrassing these days even by its creators, *Licensed To Ill* is still an astonishingly rich listening experience. There are basically three types of track on the record: the obviously rock-fixated 'Fight For Your Right' and 'No Sleep Til Brooklyn'; crazy, off-kilter asides like 'Girls' and 'Brass Monkey', where the emergent traditions of hip-hop are largely ignored in favour of schoolyard skits; and the rest, which constituted some of the finest hip-hop that had then been committed to tape.

Take the penultimate track, 'Slow And Low'. Swinging just like the title says it will, the track pitches a sonic boom of a programmed bassline into a sparse melée of sounds including that most quintessential b-boy staple, cowbells, and a sample of a motor vehicle accelerating away into the distance. A stabbing guitar powerchord is dropped into the mix preceded by a couple of scratch-like sounds (though in reality the effect is less likely to have been produced by a DJ and a record deck than by an engineer with a sampler or drum machine), emphasising the track's hip-hop style at the same time as it presents itself as rock-flavoured and more easily accessible. If *Licensed To Ill* does one thing better than anything else, it's this: making a virtue out of its non-hip-hop components and, by doing so, simultaneously increasing the album's b-boy coefficient.

Yet it's vocally where 'Slow And Low' succeeds most strongly. Exhorting the listener from the off to "Let it flow, let yourself go", the Beasties set about creating a party the teenager inside you won't want to miss out on. Echoing the techniques of the early pioneers of rap, the verses aren't split in a predictable manner between the emcees: instead, there's a dazzlingly complex interplay between the three voices, with MCA, Mike D and Adrock taking portions of lines for themselves, hollering in unison on rhyming words, taking the listener off at mad tangents and generally coming across like a cross between Kiss and the Fantastic Five. Content-wise, the track, like most of the album, is a glorious mixture of heavy-handed self-parody, inverted rap clichés and tales of adolescent beer-guzzling. "It's time to party so have a ball" is the one coherent 'message', if you could call it that.

The writing of this track (along with 'Paul Revere', it was written with the help of Run DMC) provides an interesting insight into the Beasties creative process. Speaking in 1998, Run explained "'Slow And Low' was just something they took a tape of, they heard it and they just made it over. We made it but we didn't love it, so we threw it away and they took it and made it." Although he maintains that "every lyric" is as he originally wrote it, 'Slow And Low' is still a quintessential Beasties song: and while many of the lyrics bear the unmistakable hand of the Simmons/McDaniels writing team, there is sufficient material in the lyric to suggest that the Beasties made it one of their own. Certainly the orchestration of the lyrics between the three voices could not have been engineered for Run DMC's two vocalists, and there are many lyrics that have at the very least been adapted for Beastie usage (several references to the band's name and to the three individuals are prominent without seeming to have been pasted in as an afterthought) Also, in lines like "Strong as an ox, fresh out the box/The crowd's so live they're coming in flocks", there seems to be a definably Beastie sense of humour at work.

Rap music is obsessed to the point of neurosis with being new: rarely has such a musical movement demanded such constant self-revision, and rarely, if ever, have the fans of a scene been so relentlessly neophyte. The reasons for this are complex, but are rooted in hip-hop's twin nature. It's not just a cultural form with attendant strands existing in adjacent arts to music (breakdancing and graffiti writing being essential components alongside DJ-ing and emceeing), though that in itself sets hip-hop apart: what makes it so urgently inventive is that each of these disciplines grew in a competitive environment. Even in the late '90s, when hip-hop culture is approaching middle age and record company marketing departments seem to have more say in the musical destiny of the genre than the kid in the street who makes, breaks and buys the records, there are still DJ and emcee competitions across the world, where rappers and DJs stand in front of their peers to demonstrate the range and breadth of their skills and techniques. The same goes for breakdancing, a form of physical expression that's been sneered at for years yet finds itself undergoing a phenomenal renaissance in the late '90s, and the very essence of the proliferation of graffiti rests in the competitive relationship that exists between the writers. While rock music might have the occasional 'Battle Of The Bands', such events are usually just half-hearted apologies for competition. They're really just a talent show, presided over by judges whose decisions are often entirely subjective and are usually based on an individual's appreciation of a song or a performance. At a Battle Of The Bands competition you'll see a few hopefuls going through their well-rehearsed set: go to an open mic session at your nearest hip-hop fleapit and there's everything there bar the sparks flying (though occasionally you get those as well). Hip-hop music is rooted in the call-and-response tradition that has formed the backbone of black musical heritage from African chants through blues and gospel and into the present era of (theoretically comparative) musical sophistication and complexity. Rapping is also derived from word games such as 'the dozens', where a response from the audience is integral to the performance. As rapping requires only a voice, a vocabulary and a willingness to acquire skills as a vocalist, it excludes none of its audience from potential involvement. In all the elements of hip-hop, the experts are the artists, and the known parameters of the art are constantly being re-defined: form, attitude, delivery and content all play a part, but in a rap competition the belt will go to the guy or girl who pulls something different and exciting out of the hat, something that takes the art form on another step or two. And the audience, composed of artists or potential artists, decides on this basis who is the best rapper, or who has given the best display of craft on the particular occasion concerned.

In their desire to be the newest and the best, then, the Beasties of *Licensed To Ill* are simply being b-boy to the bone. They spew hip-hop reference points to underline their authenticity but they keep you guessing about whether they actually mean any of it. MCA closes the first verse of 'Slow And Low' with what sounds like a catchphrase you've heard a million times, but on closer inspection is part of the big joke he and his group are perpetrating: "What you see is what you get/And you ain't seen nothing yet."

As with most - at least, most rock - bands making their first album, much of the material included on *Licensed To Ill* would have been performed live many times before recording. If you consider, then, that the first exposure to 'Slow And Low' many people would have had would have been live, with the Beastie Boys on stage in front of them, the above couplet takes on a different dimension to the one it seems to have at face value. There's a play on words in operation that allows the listener to interpret the song in two ways: either as a cocksure boast that the best of the Beasties is yet to come, or as an 'accidentally' self-deprecating put-down that suggests that the people in front of you on stage are "nothing", nobodies, and that there's precious little chance of any improvement. It's complex: you're invited to laugh at the Beasties' stupidity, yet you're also supposed to realise they're in on that particular joke too - and all the while, these three yapping caricatures are making some unarguably brilliant music. At its best, which is often through the thirteen tracks, *Licensed To Ill* maintains these distinct levels and functions in all its many modes simultaneously.

Hearing it live is the key to 'Slow And Low'. In London to promote their *Check Your Head* album in 1992, and before embarking on the full band live show they have today, the Beasties played a gig at the legendary London rock venue, The Marquee, as a four-piece with DJ Hurricane. This is the line-up that toured in the *Licensed To Ill* era, and, stripped of the all-encompassing chaos that enveloped them at that time, the Beasties gave a glimpse of how jaw-droppingly incredible they can be as a straight-up rap band. 'Slow And Low' started the set and the mic-passing dynamics of the track seemed to energise the three emcees. Mike D got busy conflating the traditional punk pogo dance with a couple of Michael Jordan basketball moves, jumping unfeasibly high then just hanging there, while Yauch prowled the rear of the stage, nodding almost vacantly as the groove enveloped him between his turns on the mic. Nothing? Nothing like it.

'Rhymin & Stealin', the album's opening track, follows a similar pattern to 'Slow And Low' both musically and lyrically. A massive slab of John Bonham's drumming from Led Zeppelin's 'When The Levee Breaks' is suffixed with grunting guitar riffs (this is music you can only describe as grungy, yet it was made years before the word came to denote an entire musical sub-genre) and sly, piss-taking raps. This time the Beasties critique hip-hop's sonic pilfering of musical source material and base their imagery around pirates. It's a rich metaphor for them to explore, as it allows them to merge their cartoon violence with a veritable treasure chest of easily assimilable references their audience can latch on to.

The first verse mentions *Mutiny On The Bounty*, and the old line about sixteen men on a dead man's chest before concluding in a boast of unutterably glorious dumbness that sums up the album and its themes: "I am most ill when I'm rhymin' and stealin'". The track goes on to pay jocular homage to the Three Musketeers, The Clash (a brief lift of their version of 'I Fought The Law' is sampled in the final verse), the Sex Pistols and *The Arabian Knights*. The point - that the Beasties will get really quite upset with anyone who steals the beat that they have themselves stolen, and that their retribution will involve sadistic acts of piracy that three teenage delinquents from New York are quite clearly going to be incapable of performing - proves nothing less than addictive in its all-round ludicrousness.

'Slow Ride' moves away from rigid adherence to all things metallic, half-inches the well-known brass riff from LA funksters War's 'Low Rider' hit, augments it with an almost weedy bongo pattern and stirs in lyrics further illustrating the Beasties' inimitably pathetic attempt to be "bad". They claim their neighbours have tried to have them evicted for playing their music too loud, then claim that "Being bad news is what we're all about/We went to White Castle and we got thrown out." White Castle is a low-rent chain of hamburger restaurants. A menace to society? Perhaps not.

This blend of sub-*Happy Days, Animal House* squealing brat nerdishness struck a chord with more than just the band's immediate audience: fictional characters from films and TV shows such as the *Bill And Ted* series, *Wayne's World*, *Beavis And Butthead* and *The King Of The Hill* all find antecedents in the shape of Mike D, MCA and Adrock on *Licensed To Ill*. They think they're hard; they think they're unutterably cool; yet everything they do is crass and unsuccessful. And they know it too, giving the joke a complex extra dimension.

The rest of the album largely serves to reinforce these comedic personalities, highlight Rubin's sharp, intuitive production and focus on the trio's routinely consummate rap skills. 'The New Style', 'She's Crafty' and 'Hold It Now, Hit It' are invigorating examples of the superior rap music the Beasties could make in their sleep that still sound fresh today. 'Time To Get Ill' adds samples from the theme to the ancient TV show *Mr. Ed* to the brew, while 'Paul Revere' is just plain odd.

Yet however hard you try to stay focused on the exceptional stuff that surrounds them, whenever you think of *Licensed To Ill* you keep coming back to the two rock songs at the album's core. Both released as singles, 'Fight For Your Right' and 'No Sleep Till Brooklyn' would overshadow both the album and, effectively, the Beastie Boys' whole career.

Armed with three chords and a snotty attitude, 'Fight For Your Right' became the 'Louie Louie' of the late '80s: for eighteen months it was the essential trash-the-place end-of-night anthem at pretty much every student party throughout the English-speaking world, and, for that matter, beyond. The lyrics catalogue the woes of a middle class schoolboy who lives with Mum, hates his relatively simple part in the world and wants to shout about it. The song's narrator wants to stay in bed but has to go to school, which he hates because the teacher treats him like "some kinda jerk". No surprise there, then. Dad gets some stick in verse two for telling our hero off for smoking when he "smokes two packs a day". Clearly, staying with the folks is a bit of a problem, and the situation takes a marked downturn when the Beastie finds out his Mum has chucked out his favourite porn magazine. Around and about this tale of grief and sorrow, the Beasties interject a fractured, fist-in-the-air refrain - what seems like the only way out of the troubles a chainsmoking, porn-reading, home-living schoolboy endures. "You gotta fight - for your right - to parrrr - tay!"

Subtle it ain't. But 'Fight For Your Right' had a massive captive audience. It supplied a shot in the arm to young teens depressed with the situations they were in but perhaps possessed of enough self-knowledge to realise their problems were comparatively trivial; yet it also got across on a simpler level to pretty much everybody else. The song was also vaguely well thought-of among people a bit older and - they liked to think - a bit wiser, who saw it as ironic and got into it for the same reason. The single reached No. 2 in America, a place lower in Britain, and established the band as a household name. It would also dog them for years to come, in that manner only the most insidious of hit singles can, because even people who knew nothing about the band had heard and formed an opinion about it.

'No Sleep Till Brooklyn' was the natural follow-up, though this is much more to do with its superficial musical and structural similarities to 'Fight...' than for any thematic relationship between the two tracks. Set alight with as un-minimal a gesture as a guitar solo, 'No Sleep...' utilises an almost identical style of chorus - a simple three chord guitar motif is ruptured by three shouted voices declaiming the title - but the lyrics switch this time to what the band gets up to on the road. In this, the Beasties evoke Zeppelin again, though the song's title and elements of the lyrics are derived from another British metal act - Motorhead. Another band to whom an element of wryly accepted mocking self-knowledge is integral, the awesomely loud three-piece led by Lemmy Kilminster released a live album called *No Sleep Till Hammersmith* in the mid-80s, which is clearly where the Beasties got their song's title from (Hammersmith Odeon - now the Apollo - being the London venue where Motorhead played a residency at at the end of their British tours). Lyrically there is a clear link. In 'We Are The Road Crew', a track from Motorhead's benchmark *Ace Of Spades* album, which remains a firm live favourite and appeared on the *...Hammersmith* live LP, Lemmy pays homage to the sweaty, alcohol-fuelled, sex-filled life of a roadie touring with the band. "Another town, another place/Another girl, another face/Another drug, another race..." These lyrics are clearly the inspiration for a similar passage from '...Brooklyn'. The Beasties' lines, which similarly speak of all-night drives and nameless women encountered on the road, are delivered at speed during the bridge between the chorus and the second verse of their song and are structured as a group of four lines, while Motorhead's come in threes, get enunciated much more slowly and form the song's verses. Yet the source is unmistakable.

Motorhead was an extremely clever reference for the Beasties to make. Partly because of their extreme volume but mainly because of the tremendous speed with which they played the majority of their live sets ('Road Crew' is, oddly, a poor example of this), Motorhead were the only metal band ever to be whole-heartedly embraced by punk rockers. Whether they realised it or not at the time, the Beastie Boys are responsible for, if not instigating, at least *catalysing* a reappraisal of metal among an audience weaned on punk. So by referencing Zeppelin, the Sex Pistols and Motorhead while still getting across to fans of hip-hop - the new punk - the band managed to simultaneously define themselves sharply as a singular and very, very cool group, but also as a walking, talking piss-take of themselves and the various scenes they straddled. Which, however you look at it, is a neat trick.

Released late in 1986, *Licensed To Ill* sold exceptionally quickly and met with an ecstatic, if bewildered, critical response. Writing in English music weekly *NME,* Steven Wells was repulsed by the group's apparent embrace of the sexism that plagued much metal music, but blown away by the revolutionary form of the album and its punk-like energy. He decreed the Beasties to be "Sex Zeppelin." Meanwhile, on the other side of the Atlantic, the clearest example of the dichotomies the record embodied in most reviewer's minds is provided by the headline the influential New York weekly *Village Voice* ran to accompany their review: 'Three Jerks Make A Masterpiece'. They were right on both counts.

If there's one thing that grates about *Licensed To Ill* it's that it seems keen to pander to the lowest common denominator. Yes, it's clever, it's funny, it relies on awareness of junk culture and rock/rap history to really work: but when something seems to be as insurrectionary as this, is it really enough to just be fighting "for your right to party"? What about saying something you believe in, making those anthems from the fraternity house as important as sermons from the barricades? Why, in a sense, did these punk initiates not take up the gauntlet thrown down by rebel rockers like The Clash, or translate 'Anarchy In The UK' into a north American setting? Speaking to *Playboy's* Charles Young in 1987, Adam Yauch touched on this issue.

"What most adults don't understand about most teenagers is that most teenagers are extremely conservative most of the time, even as they are engaging in obnoxious behaviour designed to differentiate themselves from most adults. Most teenagers enjoy a heavily structured life, are threatened by deviations from the conforming norm and will ridicule those enamoured of deviating from the conforming norm. In this way, most teenagers are exactly like most adults, the only difference being that teenagers piss their lives away in high school while adults piss their lives away in corporations. Most teenagers do, after all, grow up to be most adults."

Speaking as *Licensed To Ill* was about to top the American album charts, Yauch's right to pontificate seems not unreasonable. To those weaned on the all-out attack philosophies of the punk era, his views may seem profoundly distressing, but at least he could point to his success as vindication of his notions and his approach to his music. Even if this is all *Licensed To Ill* is - a reassuring shot of brattish obnoxiousness from a troupe of clever young men who've given it enough anti-establishment credibility to make their record appear dangerous to adults while remaining accessible and desirable to the sought-after teenage audience - it is still a considerable achievement. Some may even make claims for it being subversive. And a few people well placed to make such a judgement have made claims for its validity as art. Admittedly, Israel Horovitz could hardly be described as an impartial judge, but his comments to *The Los Angeles Times* are revealing.

"If people can't see the humour and satire in the record, I don't know what to say to them," Adrock's father said. "It's all so obvious. I think the thing that makes the record so good is that it shows a real understanding of people; maybe not an understanding of 49-year-olds, but certainly of 17-year-olds. I am delighted beyond description; it's like a kid taking over the family store."

Certainly, in defence of the album's nihilism, it can be argued that the record represents a startling warning to the political and social establishments that sought to have its makers hounded out of the pubic eye. If one is to try to understand the album in any serious sort of way, you have to consider its worth, as Horovitz Senior is hinting, as a piece of satirical social observation. What can we learn of adolescent America in 1986 from this record? Maybe not much we didn't already know: teenagers, as Yauch told *Playboy*, are often as reactionary and scared of change as their parents, are largely bored most of the time, play at being tough in front of their mates when in reality their insecurities prevent them from being assertive enough, and have given up on any hope that they may have a meaningful influence on their society. It is surely not mere coincidence that levels of apathy among first time voters in the United States and western Europe reached new peaks during these years. As governments in the USA and Britain, in particular, became convergent around a single political philosophy, with voter choice limited to one of two parties (Republican and Democrat, Conservative and Labour) whose defining parameters all but vanished, it seemed as though a line had been drawn in the social sands. You were either part of the consensus and happy to participate in it, or you stood on the outside with no real hope of influencing events. Youth should be a time where dreams and ideals are nurtured and encouraged, yet to many young people growing up in the so-called industrialised west in the mid- to late-80s, ideals were all too often things you sacrificed for profit, dreams nothing more than the unattainable goals of hopeless romantics. It's little wonder so many people decided to take a turn away from the way things had been done before - and even a decision to step into a mental and philosophical void seemed like a tempting move compared to the other options available. So, in adopting these caricatures and living out this fantasy lifestyle, the Beasties were actually providing *positive* role models, by seemingly proving the validity of an imagination and demonstrating that it was possible to succeed on the older generation's terms - i.e. financially - by making a virtue out of what they sought to take away from you.

This point was never fully appreciated at the time, though, and the rather more dubious parts of the band's package were allowed to overshadow the whole. It's interesting to note that similar mistakes of appreciation and perception are still being made: for example, most discussion of *Be Here Now*, the third album by Manchester rock band Oasis - routinely described through the mid-90s, like the Beasties before them, as "the bad boys of rock" - concentrated on its deficiencies or otherwise sonically and the band's failure to radically alter the formula of their earlier records. Yet in its lyrics, the album offers messages of hope and an encouragement to dream and keep positive in the face of institutionalised apathy: "Say something, shout it from the rooftops off your head" (from 'It's Getting Better (Man!)') may well prove to be as defining a lyric to the present generation as Bob Dylan's 'Blowin' In The Wind' had been three decades earlier, precisely because of the song's helpless lack of specificity.

If, however, the Beasties were worried about such misinterpretation, they didn't show it. They went out of their way to play the characters they'd created to the full at every available opportunity. They may have found baiting journalists and media folk to have been an eminently enjoyable pastime, but their irritation in later years about how their "ironic" act was taken seriously when it should have been seen through would have held more water had their role playing not been so convincing. They certainly seemed to have most of their interviewers believing the fiction: the following examples are merely the tip of a big phallic iceberg.

Later in the *Playboy* piece he'd proven so adroit in, Yauch tells a story about a putative Beasties porn movie: "We got a great segment of this girl who wouldn't suck dick unless we sang 'Brass Monkey'. So we sang 'Brass Monkey' and she blew us. [This happened in] Washington or Montana. Middle America, man - you'd be amazed... the South is known for its incredible dick-sucking abilities."

Speaking to *NME*'s Don Watson at the tail end of 1985, Yauch, again, was even more animated. Watson spent the interview trying to ascertain what, if anything, the band was trying to get across to its audience. MCA told him in no uncertain terms. "Basically what we are saying is that the Beastie Boys like fucking women with big floppy tits and nipples like omelettes."

Equally disturbingly, Adrock demonstrated to the same magazine a year later a rather too convincing homophobic streak. His rant against homosexuals in a Steven Wells interview in *NME* ("This is the gay area and I've lived here all my life and I *hate* faggots. I really do...I shouldn't have said that. I've got a lot of gay friends but...you don't know what it's like growing up in this neighbourhood") is a little more difficult to pass off as part of an act, for three reasons. Firstly, the widely reported working title of *Licensed To Ill* was apparently *Don't Be A Faggot:* even in their burning desire to provoke, somebody evidently realised this was perhaps not a smart idea. Secondly, if Adrock's speech was part of an act it seems odd that he should have begun to back-track - surely the people his caricature was supposed to have been ridiculing wouldn't have tried to retract such a statement? (The fact that he chooses to use the tried and tested methodology by which bigots generally justify their prejudices - "I've got a lot of gay friends" is somewhere near "I'm not a racist, I just don't like black people" - is either an incredibly subtle part of the characterisation, a weak attempt at a justification or a cringing acknowledgement that the joke had gone too far.) Finally, MCA felt the need to try to play down his band mate's comments: "Yo! Adam! We do not need to go into that. What Adam's talking about - I'll give you this, he definitely hates gay people - but the reason for that is that in this neighbourhood, when you're five years old, when you're walking down the street a lot of 'disgusting' faggots who hang around here aren't like *just* gay people - normal gay people - all the sickos who are gay hang out on Christopher Street and they see kids and they walk up to them and they say 'Hey kid, I'll give you five bucks if you suck my dick', y'know?"

"When we're talking about women or whatever, we're creating a fantasy," Yauch continued. "What we're doing is creating a fantasy so far-fetched and overboard that the 99 per cent of the people that understand it, understand that there is such a thing as humour, such a thing as parody. Most people who seem intelligent to me, they get the joke and they think it's *funny*...but when I meet people who are really *stooopid*, they either agree with the lyric or they fail to see the humour." His explanation failed to cut it with interviewer Steven Wells, who implied that their attitudes were genuine ones hiding behind a mask of supposed irony. He was not alone.

"You've just got to look at [*Licensed*] as a piece of fiction," MCA told British rap mag *Hip-Hop Connection* years later. "Like a movie. Same way you see a bunch of people shooting each other, burning down villages and shooting heroin. It's not real - it's just some ill shit. Parts of it were pretty radically exaggerated, there's definitely things in there about smoking dust and raping and pillage - which is shit we do all the time now - but at the time we hadn't started doing it. You know what I'm saying?"

"The only thing that upsets me is that we might have reinforced certain values of some people in our audience when our own values were actually totally different," Diamond would later claim in *The Independent On Sunday*. "There were tons of guys singing along to 'Fight For Your Right To Party' who were oblivious to the fact it was a total goof on them. Irony is oft missed."

What *is* deeply ironic - and unmissable - is how a band from whom such despicable statements could so casually slip (whether jocular or not) would end up being revered as one of the most socially progressive pop culture acts in the world. The 180 degree turn the Beastie Boys would eventually make away from the offensive stereotype they played out during the *Licensed...* era is little short of magnificent. With hindsight, their plan worked a treat, winding up everyone from ordinarily well-disposed liberals to reactionary conservatives, securing them acres of media coverage and helping to sell record-breaking quantities of their debut album. But it also gave them a mountain to climb when they finally realised they may have been somewhat irresponsible. It was, however, a peak they would eventually scale ("It's not even enough to say we're not homophobic," Mike D expounded to *Alternative Press'* Joe Clark in 1994. "You have to go the next step and say we're actually anti-homophobic and pro-gay. It makes me cringe if I think there's some guy with a Beastie Boys hat driving down the street saying, 'Hey, fuck you, faggots!' That's not how we live our lives"). Hindsight, though, is one of many things denied the mortal, and it's only really with its benefit that the fundamental flaw in the largely impeccable edifice the band had constructed could be seen. The only thing that could possibly go wrong for the Beastie Boys at this point in time, of course, was *everything*.

CHAPTER THREE

"What makes us significant is we're a white rap group, and we're performing for this audience that's never seen people like us."
Mike D, 1987

"Hip-hop was never about black or white," says the music's legendary innovator Kool Herc. "It was all about partying, about everyone getting together. A lot of the original b-boys were Hispanic." Herc should know - he invented hip-hop. During the mid-70s at a series of parties in the Bronx, New York, the towering Jamaican expatriate realised his crowds loved dancing to instrumental sections of records like The Incredible Bongo Band's percussion-heavy reading of the Jerry Lordan instrumental 'Apache' (better known from The Shadows' Stratocaster-soaked version), and he decided it was his job to prolong their ecstasy. Using a second copy of the same record, he replayed the instrumental break on the second turntable as soon as the same segment of music had ended on the first. These chunks became known as "break beats" ("beats" since they were largely little more than drum solos, "break" referring to the fact that the beats came from the instrumental break section of the record) and the crowd that followed Herc from club to club, party to party, became known as "break boys" and girls (terms quickly abbreviated to "b-boys" and "b-girls"). Surely if anyone knows about the original racial implications this new musical culture had, it's Herc.

The Beastie Boys were far from being the cultural pirates they have often been portrayed as. And, rather than being seen as such by the black creators of the hip-hop form, the band's race is only of importance because their involvement in rap helped bring the music to white ears for the first time. The phenomenal success they were poised to enjoy was the result of a combination of intelligent management, intuitive marketing and the band's fortuitous appearance as a fabulously talented and unique product of their place and time. But in order to understand the role the Beasties played, and how they were accepted by and large as innovators rather than imitators, some understanding of the state of hip-hop in the mid-80s is required.

At the time the Beastie Boys made their first rap records, hip-hop was still a decidedly underground scene. The majority of the records that were coming out were still in the main produced by independent companies who had a thorough understanding of the audience they were aiming to sell to, yet there was still considerable scope to wonder at the authenticity of the rap that was then making it onto vinyl.

The first rap records had been made late in the previous decade, The Fatback Band's B-side, 'King Tim III: Personality Jock' beating the much more widely known 'Rapper's Delight' by the Sugarhill Gang to the record racks by a matter of weeks in 1979. 'Rapper's Delight' is perhaps the most celebrated example of the exploitative state of the early rap "industry". Released by the Sugarhill label, owned and operated by music entrepreneur Sylvia Robinson, 'Rapper's Delight' succeeded in capturing much of the essence of the era and provided a fine indication of what rap music was about. But the Sugarhill Gang were a manufactured group put together by Robinson to cash in on hip-hop's then unexploited potential. The trio were figures peripheral to the scene rather than at its focus, but they were well-tutored. Big Bank Hank, a nightclub doorman, had his rhymes written for him by Cold Crush Brothers' Grandmaster Caz, whose own records would not be released until much later. Caz, a graffiti artist who drifted into rapping via DJ-ing, was simply one of many pioneers who received scant recognition for his talents until the mid-90s, when a resurgence of interest in rap's roots enabled him to make steps to resurrect his career and get paid for the innovations he'd made. At the British Fresh '97 festival, held nearly twenty years after the fact, Caz showed a new generation of rap fans what might have been, rapping his 'Rapper's Delight' rhymes over DJ Charlie Chase's cut-up of Chic's 'Good Times' single. That it was to take him two decades to be acknowledged for his role perhaps says enough on its own about how true the early rap labels were to the talent they fed off. (One point of note is that although the music for 'Rapper's Delight' was inspired by and almost identical to the Chic grooves, Sylvia Robinson had shown considerable foresight by anticipating later debates about sampling and copyright, and had instituted a Sugarhill house band who played the music in the studio, and aimed to replicate the sounds on the records the early DJs were cutting up. That band - Skip McDonald, Doug Wimbush and Keith LeBlanc - would later form part of the similarly influential dub-based On-U Sound label and musical movement in England.)

Partly as an attempt to redress the imbalance regarding situations like Grandmaster Caz's, and partly fuelled by the feverish desire to document a culture moving so fast it seemed in danger of slipping away, avant garde New York movie-maker Charlie Ahearn and Fab 5 Freddy began work in 1979 on a film, *Wild Style*. Not released until 1983, *Wild Style* has its limitations as a piece of filmic art; however, its depiction and description of the early days of hip-hop have elevated it to classic status among connoisseurs of the old school. It might seem surprising, but among the classic scenes of Cold Crush battling the Fantastic Five on a basketball court, beside indelible images of Grandmaster Flash cutting up records on a sideboard in his kitchen, there are clues as to why the Beastie Boys - three Jewish teenagers with a bratty image and impeccable rhyme skills - would become accepted in an almost exclusively non-white culture where "keeping it real" was always the cornerstone value.

"When I was making the movie, I felt that culture in New York was really divisive," remembers Ahearn. "The rap scene was absolutely black at that time. You had a punk/new wave scene in Manhattan clubs that was absolutely white. And I felt that there was this potential of hip-hop to liberate everyone from this whole race thing. The graffiti scene was always very mixed: more than anything else this was the thing that tied the city together, in lots of ways. Because of the nature of the subway line, the way it would run from the top of the Bronx through Manhattan and on to Brooklyn and Queens, it metaphorically and in reality tied the city together. One of the claims a [graffiti] writer would make was to call himself 'All City', which meant that his stuff was [visible] in every borough. And the easiest way to get All City was to write on the trains. If you only wrote on a building you were stuck in your own neighbourhood, but when graffiti went onto the trains, it went all over the city and it connected everybody. It connected rich people and poor people, black people and white people, it connected uptown with downtown, and whether people liked it or not, that's the world. So in a sense, that was a great opener for the whole thing. There was definitely a tremendous synergy when people from different groups - Puerto Ricans, blacks, punks - when they started hanging out together in the clubs and their culture started bringing them together, there was this tremendous amount of excitement. The whole thing was just like an explosion of art in New York city on all levels. There was breakdancing scenes happening in art galleries; uptown kids were going to clubs in Manhattan; and suddenly, where a club would have had 200 people, it had 2,000 people. And there'd be people out in the street. You'd go to an art gallery or a club and you couldn't get in, and for blocks around there'd be people who couldn't get in hanging outside on cars and there'd be tremendous energy and excitement - people didn't even care about getting inside, you just had to be there. And so there was this sort of explosion of new energy."

Chris Stein, guitarist and songwriter with Blondie, was probably the first established white musician to get involved in the hip-hop phenomenon. Like Ahearn, he'd been introduced to the scene by Fab 5 Freddy, and ended up collaborating on music for the *Wild Style* soundtrack. Blondie's 1982 hit 'Rapture' wasn't exactly a rap record, but it illustrated the group's excitement at the whole thing. Stein was itching to be involved, but felt that a certain degree of sensitivity was required. "To me, rap is heavily bound up with black culture because it's always been about black kids finding their voice," he ponders today. "It's like all these kids suddenly talking on a mass level - it's a symbolism, it's more than just music. Being white makes it a little trickier to address the whole thing and come off politically correct."

Into this potentially volatile situation stepped Rubin and Simmons. Crucially - and here's where the roots of their success lie, whether deliberate or accidental - they understood the wider potential of this music. Seeing the way New York's boho-art set and the post-punk crowd had taken to hip-hop's visceral excitement, the duo and their new Def Jam label started to address selling hip-hop music to an audience beyond the boundaries of those limited New York ghetto parameters. Controlling their own manufacturing and distribution, Def Jam had a declared agenda. "The purpose of this company is to educate people as to the value of real street music," Simmons told US trade magazine *Billboard*, "by putting out records that nobody in the business would distribute but us."

Simmons was already a respected manager, whose Rush stable was home to acts like Whodini, Kurtis Blow and, of course, Run DMC. Rubin's reputation as a producer had been forged with his very first recording - a single called 'It's Yours', by former Treacherous Three vocalist T-La Rock. Many people have strong memories of when they first heard it, though few, perhaps, as vivid as Fab 5 Freddy.

"I was at the Roxy one night and this record came on," the man born Frederick Braithwaite recollects, "and I just stopped in mid-conversation and I was like, 'What the fuck is this?' The emcee was T-La Rock from the Treacherous Three, but it was the feel…that ill, dusty feel, was just - oh my God! I felt like I was at a jam up in the park! I looked towards the DJ, thinking, 'Who's on the turntable?' Trying to find out what was playing. So I moved out onto the dancefloor, and I could see it was Bambaataa on the turntables, and I was like, 'Yo! Bam! What's that?' And he says, 'It's some new shit!' I was like 'Who made it? Who made it?' and he pointed down to this guy - there was like six or seven black guys and one white guy. I said, 'No, it can't be the white guy'. I went down to talk to him and I said, 'You made this?' He said 'Yeah.' I said, 'Who're you?' He said, 'I'm Rick Rubin'. So I said, 'Yo! We gotta talk!'"

Braithwaite maintains that it was this aural sensibility that ensured groups like Run DMC - who, as natives of Queens, were unknowns among the Bronx hip-hop community - and the Beastie Boys were held in high esteem by their contemporaries, many of whom would have otherwise been dismissive of rappers who hadn't followed their own paths through the outdoor parties and on the stages of certain clubs where the music first emerged. The reactions of rap's veterans to the newcomers were almost uniformly positive, he maintains, because the sound of the records showed the old school pioneers that they weren't encountering another Sugarhill-like manufactured exploitation scenario.

"The problem for me and for those who saw hip-hop and knew what it was supposed to be, based on the essence of having been to those park jams, was this," Freddy explains. "Those Sugarhill records were good but they weren't really capturing the elusive element, that something you really can't fuckin' describe, but you can feel it when the record is right. The Sugarhill records were just replaying what people were rapping over in the streets, but they had to use bands - good bands - but it just didn't capture the element. But Run and them just brought it fuckin' *home*."

"At that moment," Ahearn continues, referring to the time filming for *Wild Style* began, "'Rapper's Delight' was the only commercial rap single. So these guys [the original rap groups who at the time remained unrecorded] felt kinda chipped. They felt that the commercial thing had taken off and left them behind. Then, about a year after the film came out, you had Run DMC and the Beastie Boys. Their records were much better produced and they were better marketed, and they made a tremendous amount of money very fast. They were the first groups that made it really big. They were marketed in a way that could go out in to the suburbs, and they were the first phenomenon where rap started to cross over. And that's where the line was drawn between the old school and the new school."

Image, too, was vital, and Run DMC, through Russell, had learned that particular lesson early on. "The important thing to understand is that the way they looked in the beginning was the way tough guys used to look," continues Braithwaite. "Classic hardrock, player kinda guys used to dress in those leather blazers, Godfather hats, those sneakers. But originally they [Run DMC] wanted to dress up like Flash and them, and they wanted to be like Rick James or Bootsy Collins 'cos that was the biggest groups at the time. But Russell - that was part of his genius - he said 'No'. He was able to see those elements and capitalise, and force them to wear, and stay in, this one kind of outfit."

"They taught everyone the lessons of hip-hop," he remembers, encompassing both image and sound in his reappraisal of Run DMC's role. "They taught everybody, 'Hey, this is how the records should be.' Coupled with what [Grandmaster] Flash did on 'Adventures On The Wheels Of Steel', it was like, 'Hey, these are the real elements, this is what we need to be doing'. They just captured it, and from there everybody learned. The Beasties were able to figure out what that element was and how to build around it and take that shit on to another level, and just recreate the attitude of those jams."

Simmons, then, already understood how important the

Beasties could be: they were white and since he'd had no little success in selling Run DMC to the suburbs, he should be able to have a field day with the Beasties. So he took pains to give his marketable young protegés a secure foothold in the hip-hop domain. There are bound to be problems in any business relationship like the one Simmons and the Beastie Boys had: as their manager, Simmons' job was to get the best deals for his artists both financially and in terms of marketing and support from their record label. Yet with Simmons simultaneously being co-owner of the label the band were signed to, an unresolvable dichotomy existed which would eventually help to end the Beasties' links to both Rush Management and Def Jam. But for all its disadvantages, the arrangement at least meant that Simmons was entirely focused on ensuring the Beasties were set up to achieve the greatest possible commercial success. His stewardship of their emerging months can hardly be faulted.

"Certainly, every phenomenon is a convergence of elements at a certain moment, and these guys can't escape their historical moment," offers Bill Adler. "I will say in general, though, that the Beasties, like the rest of the Rush artists, benefited from having management, which is why LL Cool J and Run DMC are still around. It is really hard in the rap business to sustain a career. One of the reasons for this is [that they had] effective management, which was not always true of most of the artists who recorded on other labels. That doesn't take anything away from the Beasties - they came into the game with a sense of solidarity, but they certainly benefitted from that management. Russell would make sure that they were marketed so as not to be taken by the black community as novelty. They were not, and they were not *going* to be, Vanilla Ice five years early, and that was very much because of Russell's management planning."

Because of the excitement picked up on by the likes of Ahearn and Stein, and because of the speed at which the music and the culture were moving, hip-hop seemed ripe for assimilation and absorption into mainstream - that is, white - culture. Like rock and roll before the emergence of Elvis Presley, all hip-hop needed in 1986 was a saleable white band doing it half-competently for a conservative music industry to cash in. And if this is all that the Beastie Boys had been, or if it was all they had been seen to be, their success would have been transient and their impact minimal. One needs only to examine the truncated careers of minimally skilled white rappers such as Vanilla Ice, or the tracksuited suburbanite-to-tattooed hoodlum *volte-face* of House Of Pain's Everlast to see that the values that matter in hip-hop are unyieldingly those of the street. White kids shelling out for a Beastie Boys record were buying more than the latest manifestation of rock or punk (although they were getting that, too) - they were buying into a culture that was streetwise, credible and cool, but which had previously remained largely inaccessible. Consequently, if Rubin, the Beasties or Def Jam had no credibility with rap audiences the purchase of a Beasties album by a white teenager only dimly aware of rap music and hip-hop culture would have been significantly diminished. Bill Adler was well placed to witness Simmons' management tactics at first hand. He sees the emergent mogul's priority in establishing the Beasties as a band with credibility in the hip-hop world as being fundamental to their future crossover success.

"Russell's idea was always, 'We don't make records, we build artists'," Adler recalls. "That was his motto at Rush Management, and so the whole thing was of artist development and then record sales under the umbrella of a career of an artist. And he applied that to the Beasties as well. Russ provided the Beasties with street credibility."

In the summer of 1986, Run DMC toured the USA to support the release of their *Raising Hell* album. Fellow Rushtown clients LL Cool J and Whodini were part of the bill, and first on stage every night was the Beastie Boys. "This was a hardcore rap tour, they played arenas, so the crowds ranged from ten to twenty thousand a night and it was almost exclusively a young black crowd," Adler remembers. "All the other artists were black, and then there were these crazy white kids, the Beasties. Because of the kind of cool way that Russ built them up - 'Here they are, they're Rush artists in the way that Whodini, LL and Run DMC are Rush artists, they're touring with us, what do you think of them?' - there was no trumpeting of them as white, they weren't placed as a novelty at all, these were just kids who had their own skills and their own sound and they belonged on this tour. And that built up tremendous credibility in the black community."

Adler describes the Beasties' appearance on the *Raising Hell* tour as "absolutely crucial" to ensuring their credibility and securing a firm base from which to launch a pop career. But Simmons wasn't content to go part of the way and leave the job half done: there were many obstacles still to be negotiated, including the over-enthusiasm of a major label whose agenda was less long-term than Russell would have liked.

"At the end of '86, Columbia heard 'Fight For Your Right' and they flipped," says Adler. "They said, 'We have a huge pop - meaning white - record here. Rock radio will play this record in a way that they have never played any rock records made by rap artists previously, because those artists had the 'misfortune' of being black'. But the Beasties were white and had made a rock record. Columbia was salivating. Columbia's idea was not even 'Fuck the black audience'. It was '*What* black audience?' And Russ was like, 'Fuck you, I've spent a lot of time building up their credibility with the black audience and we can't ignore that.' So they dropped two singles at the same time."

"The singles went to black radio for a couple of weeks, but then there was just no way to contain Columbia's enthusiasm, and it went to white radio and, boom! It went the fuck up and became a No. 1 single. Russ had taken time to establish them with young black kids, so when that record sold six to seven million copies worldwide and quickly went double platinum,

I think that some very large part of that the first couple of million was young black kids - after that, mostly white kids.

"They got over to white kids because in their own mind they were the '80s version of Led Zeppelin or Johnny Rotten. But they were about excess, destruction in their personal lives and careers, and that was a very potent thing in the middle of the '80s when there were all these hair bands dominating TV, and everything had got very safe, very packaged, very corny. So in contrast, the Beasties were this great gust of fresh air. They brought a street look back into rock 'n' roll, they weren't packaged: that was something else Russ did for them. Very early on, when they were making the transition from so-called punk rock to rap, they bought these very fancy tracksuits and sneakers and they just tried to be the white Run DMC. That lasted about a week. Russ said, 'No! You're not Run DMC, my brother is Run DMC, and you're gonna be seen as fake'. Russ' aesthetic then was [all about] what's fake and what's real and he judged everything by those standards, and if you were fake you were over. So he could not let the Beasties be fake. How did he make the Beasties real? Well, how do they go around every day? Jeans, baseball caps, trainers - fine, that's how they're gonna be on stage. Russ gave them that freedom to be themselves on stage. It was kind of a college kid look, a punk rock look: 'We wear jeans and T-shirts and [when we] go on stage, we're just like you'. Russ put them back on that track. That distinguished them next to Run DMC and the other black artists, and then as soon as they busted on to MTV, it stood them in stark contrast to what was going on in rock 'n' roll at that time."

So the Beastie Boys took rap to a rock audience because they had learned from Russell and Run DMC about how to package the music and make it exciting, and because they happened to have the good fortune to come along at a time when, with the MTV sponsored pre-eminence of bands like Bon Jovi, Van Halen and Whitesnake, too little mainstream rock music offered anything stimulating or dangerous. And yet, as the first white rappers, it fell to them to ensure the mistakes made in earlier eras over acknowledging the black roots of the music they were making weren't repeated. For the first visible white rap band to have come across as an industry-inspired cash-in would have been disastrous for all concerned, in no small part because that's exactly how they would have been perceived. Compared to the people who bought into the notion that Elvis "invented" rock and roll, music buyers of the mid- to late-80s were an altogether more sophisticated breed, one fully aware of the histories of both black and white popular music, schooled by a plethora of magazine, TV and radio outlets, used to assimilating torrents of information at a considerably faster rate. The Beasties and the machinery around them had to convince a public that would have been able to see through artifice easily. In short, they had to be *good*.

In a 1996 interview in *Institute for Labour and Mental Health, Tikkun*, Adam Yauch remembered what it was like for the band to be the first white rappers on record, and his comments underline one unspoken fundamental: the Beastie Boys achieved their credibility to a black audience by virtue of their skills as rappers first and foremost.

"When our first hip-hop records came out ['Rock Hard' etc], there weren't really any other white kids out rhyming. It's possible that there might have been other white kids who rhymed at block parties or whatever, but if so, it was a rare occurrence and they weren't making records. So, when we started making hip-hop records, it hit first in the black community before it did at all with the white kids. Most white kids outside of New York had never heard of hip-hop. At the time, a lot of people, having just heard the music, thought we were black. When people finally met us and saw that we were white, they were surprised, not that we sounded black, but just because it was out of left field to have somebody rhyming who was white. It wasn't until later when *Licensed To Ill* came out and 'Fight For Your Right To Party' that it started to flip to a white audience. At the time, a lot of hip-hop lyrics spoke about unity between the races. There was little or no racial tension in hip-hop."

"I'm thinking, 'How did they get over to these black kids?'," Adler muses. "They did it because they made very credible hip-hop/rap records. And they managed to get over and establish themselves as a viable creative force amongst black kids without sounding conventionally black. They got over because they had that attitude, Rick made def beats for them, they were very funny, they were very steeped in the argot of black youth and they had these crazy rhyme skills. The thing about the Beasties is that you can go and sneer at them, but if you lay their stuff, their lyrics, out on the page...well, it's pretty remarkable. These guys can write."

"I think to the credit of Def Jam, they came in with the right idea," Ahearn sums up. "When they came up with their idea of marketing rap they came in with Run DMC and the Beastie Boys. Run DMC did a lot to market themselves to suburban whites, and I think the Beastie Boys themselves did a lot to break down [racial] barriers. So I don't think those groups were divisive. I would say they helped [heal] racial divisions rather than cause them."

Which perhaps goes some way towards explaining why so many segments of Western established society decided the Beastie Boys posed some sort of threat. Many artists since have pointed to the crossover of rock and rap as something that makes social institutions feel uncomfortable, since much social conditioning and training depends on people being separated from one another and kept in smaller, more manageable numbers. From Sham '69's simplistic and optimistic observation that "If the kids are united they will never be divided" through to politicised LA rapper Ice-T's detailed analyses of the processes of racial politics and social control, as evinced in his book, *The Ice Opinion,* that lead him to believe it's in the interests of the powers that be to divide and keep separate youth groups of different ethnicities, the message remains the same: the mixing of rap and rock music leads to their audiences intermingling, and there are those in positions of power and authority who don't wish to see this happen. As conspiracy theories go, this one seems pretty clear cut.

When the Beasties and Run DMC toured the US together in 1987, the panic was widespread. Run DMC had headlined a show in Long Beach, California, the previous year where around 40 people were injured in what appeared to be an outbreak of violence between members of rival gangs in the audience. The media linked the violence to rap music, yet the incident was in fact related to Los Angeles' then still little-known but nevertheless enormous gang war (as detailed in Sanyika Shakur's book *Monster, The Autobiography of an LA Gang Member,* which traces such gang violence back as early as the 1960s). It had taken place in the auditorium before Run DMC had gone on stage, and the other 64 dates on the tour went ahead without incident, yet the notion that the group "inspired" violence among audiences stuck with the media, authority figures and, consequently, anxious parents. Writing in *The Detroit Free Press* about a Run DMC/Beastie Boys show in Cincinnati, John D. Gonzalez sketched a history to the tension and quoted police sources in advance of the concert, as well as speaking to gig-goers afterwards. His conclusions speak volumes.

Noting the police's desire to cancel the gig in advance for what appeared to have been subjective reasons of musical taste (local Chief of Police Lawrence Whalen is quoted as saying, "We have information from 20 other cities indicating that this act [the Beasties] is garbage"), Gonzales reports that the concert passed off without incident and that the bands sought to promote racial unity throughout the event. "We don't encourage violence. We don't encourage gang riots. And we don't like it when we hear people say those things about us," Gonzales quotes DMC as saying, before deciding that "In fact, the Beastie Boys, who are white, and Run-DMC, who are black, see their combined tour as promoting racial harmony by bringing white audiences and black audiences together: 'Elvis

Presley never toured with Chuck Berry,' McDaniels said."

Bill Adler went to the cities where the panic was most evident to try and get these sorts of points across. "That [tour] was something that seemed to generate a lot of hysteria and fear in the heartland, and I remember in Portland and Cincinnati the town's fathers were trying to ban the Beasties, so I went out on the road and held press conferences before the show. I would say, in effect, 'Listen, here are the Beasties and Run DMC, your fears are completely exaggerated, and I'm gonna make a bold prediction that they are gonna pay the local arena tonight and it will not be in smoking ruins by the end.'"

Gonzales noted the racial mix of the audience in Cincinnati. "There were white people who knew every song by Run DMC," he wrote, "and black people who were singing every lyric with the Beastie Boys. 'Look around you,' said [concert-goer] Patrick Todd. 'This is great. There's black and white people having fun together. This is the way it should be, together forever.'"

Mike D echoed these observations in a contemporaneous interview with *Rock And Soul*. "We have the most mixed group of fans of any tour out there," he told writer Scott Mehno. "We get an equal share of black kids and white kids, which is what is so great about rap and rock merging."

Ultimately, the results of the Beastie Boys' successful capturing of the two audiences would help to produce a profound sea-change in the lifestyle patterns of young America. In a later piece in *Newsday*, journalist Frank Owen came as close as anyone has to successfully analysing the group's importance as harbingers of a possible new era in race relations. "Rather than 'exploiting' black culture, the Beastie Boys are an example of what academic and writer Cornel West calls 'the Afro Americanisation of American youth'," he wrote. "White kids sporting leather Africa medallions. Black youths wearing Doc Martens. Rappers fronting hard-core bands. We live in times where white youths, knowing their parents' culture is bankrupt, are increasingly turning to their black counterparts for advice on everything from fashion to politics. Public Enemy rapper Chuck D expresses surprise at the depth of knowledge that many white teenagers he meets have about figures like Malcolm X. It's unlikely that frat party anthems like 'Fight for Your Right to Party' and 'No Sleep Till Brooklyn' turned many white kids into Black Muslims, but they did introduce rap to hard rock's mass audience. Thanks in part to the groundbreaking work done by the Beastie Boys, it's now possible to talk of a 'new whiteness' developing in young America. Not Norman Mailer's old 'White Negro' journeying to the heart of the ghetto in search of the exotic and erotic, but a new sensibility that is born not out of racial self-hatred, but of the belief that black culture has something to teach whites."

The group's legacy, then, would have been considerable even had they failed to make it beyond album number one. What visionaries like Ahearn and Simmons saw as hip-hop's potential, the Beastie Boys helped turn into a reality. Yet for the B-Boys, this was only the beginning.

CHAPTER FOUR

"It wasn't until 'Fight For Your Right To Party' came out that we started acting like drunken fools. At that point, our image shifted in a different direction, maybe turning off the kids that were strictly into hip-hop. It started out as a goof on that college mentality, but then we ended up personifying it."
Adam Yauch

Touring to support a No. 1 album should've been a breeze. When the Beastie Boys headed out on the road with Run DMC in what is still possibly the biggest rap package tour in the history of the music, it looked like another inspired move by Simmons on behalf of his charges. A triumphal procession across America was one thing, but by the time the two bands reached the UK the situation had changed.

A short series of dates at three to five thousand capacity venues across Britain during May 1987 was announced, and the majority of the shows sold out quickly. A night at Liverpool's Royal Court Theatre, among a batch added later in response to heavy ticket demand, and one of only a couple of dates on the tour's British leg without Run DMC, was the principal exception. At this point in time, the Beasties were not the bigger draw to UK audiences: a combination of tabloid hysteria and music press over-reaction to the violence at rap concerts in the US, and the linkage made between the music and the activities of street gangs, managed to put off many curious outsiders: and to die-hard rap fans (even in 1987 there were significant numbers of them in Britain) Run DMC were significantly more important than the Beasties.

"We wasn't wild, crazy - we wasn't a story you could sell as big," reasons Run, attempting eleven years later to assess why his band weren't as caught up in the media spotlight as his friends and touring partners. "They created the name 'Beastie' - pretty scary. They had some wilder props on the stage and [the press] was makin' up lies about 'em. Our story I guess, while we was great musically, our story wasn't as notorious or as cover-worthy. Musically we were good, but crazy we were not. They could sell more papers saying 'the Beastie Boys turned over cars' and what not. And on stage they were a little wilder, drinkin' beer and throwin' it on each other. It was a different vibe they were trying to sell: this sex and violence vibe [came from] the media."

Contrary to the fans' perspectives, the substantial advance press for the UK tour concerned the Beastie Boys almost exclusively. And, in common with most of the British popular press' reporting of youth cultural movements, almost everything written about the band prior to their arrival in Britain was ill-informed and alarmist. At this time the band's stage show was, like their records, part of a plan to calculatedly offend. A go-go dancer and former stripper, Eloise, appeared on stage with the group, in various states of undress, usually in a cage. The three rappers would habitually prowl the stage armed with cans of lukewarm beer that they spent more time spraying on the audience and one another than drinking. The brewing company took exception to the fact that the band performed occasionally in front of a large Budweiser logo, so they stopped using the backdrop. This seemed a little unfair: after all, the band were using an awful lot of their product. The brewers clearly didn't like the public associating Budweiser too closely with a bunch of pissed-up adolescent oiks.

"Everything we did was stupid," Mike D told Q magazine's Howard Johnson in 1996. "When we were asked what kind of stage show we wanted the first thing we could think of was a giant dick, so we had one made! It seemed the obvious thing to do at the time. We used the dick down in Alabama and Carolina and completely freaked everyone out. We were immediately banned and they passed a Beastie Boys Ordnance outlawing outrageous and immoral behaviour in a public place. This was where the British tabloids first picked up on us."

Details of the band's performances on the *Raising Hell* tour were exaggerated from their already cartoonish proportions and splashed across acres of British newsprint. By the time the tour hit Europe, tales of the band's "outrageous" shows, liberally sprinkled with sex and alcohol, had become the stuff of Fleet Street legend. The tabloid press love a band like the Beasties were then; to describe their tour as being eagerly awaited by the media would have been a considerable understatement. Yet press reporting of the band didn't merely fan the flames of a volatile situation: it effectively provided the fuel for the fire and lit the match as well.

The British press has long exuded a veneer of youthful exuberance used to maintain an illusion that it is in touch with the feelings of the majority of the right-minded citizens it seeks to sell newspapers to. But in reality, the various daily titles are often mouthpieces for their proprietors, whose vested interests are promoted *ad nauseum* and who habitually side with a little-England mentality that fears and distrusts change, seeks to shore up so-called "traditional" values in life, art and society and runs screaming with indignation and incomprehension from anything that threatens the *status quo*. Normally, this is restricted to political reporting, which is usually heavily slanted to support the party the newspaper's owner favours, but occasionally the reporting of a youth cultural phenomenon is used to reinforce the newspaper's standing in the eyes of what it believes is its readership. The mid-market tabloid papers in Britain predominantly support an old-style conservatism that would find anything like the Beastie Boys anathema: the mock horror espoused in the writing of the likes of *The Daily Express* and *Daily Mail* was therefore unsurprising. Similarly unlikely to raise eyebrows, but certainly more self-contradictory to anyone unfamiliar with the British media, was the wave of outrage that drenched the band from the tabloids. *The Sun* and *The Daily Star* were apoplectic in their indignation that the band should have stage props such as a 25-foot hydraulically-operated penis and skimpily attired go-go dancers in cages on stage, while remaining oblivious to the double standard they were operating by printing pictures of topless women on page three of their rags every day. As analysed by Sarah Thornton in her dissection of the way the tabloid press switched from attacking to utilising rave music for their own ends a couple of years later, the contrariness of these newspapers seems to know no bounds. Thornton's essay, 'Moral Panic, the Media and British Rave Culture', notes that "in Britain, the best guarantee of radicality is rejection by one or both of the disparate institutions seen to represent the cultural *status quo*: the tempered, state-sponsored BBC...and the sensational, sales-dependent tabloids." One only has to glance at the tabloids during a major international football tournament to comprehend their obliviousness to what they're doing: during the European Championships of 1996, when the England team played both Spain and Germany, several papers were rebuked by press watchdogs for the xenophobic tone of their pre-match writing ('Achtung! Surrender!' was the *Mirror*'s front page headline on the day England played Germany). Yet when these tabloid-fed chickens come home to roost, and violence erupts involving English so-called 'fans', it's the same papers that rush to condemn the thugs' behaviour, even though their jingoism has helped to foster the cultural atmosphere in which such attitudes can breed.

It was into this illogical ferment of reactionary bullshit and media frenzy that the Beasties stepped, improperly prepared for what was about to occur. Their main mistake was in believing that the audience they would play to would all be in on the joke they had created - an illusion abruptly shattered by beer cans and baseball bats a few days later. Even the indignation and offence they were deemed to have caused during their tour of the US with Madonna two years earlier was nothing compared to this.

By the time the group's UK appearances began to draw near, tabloid fury was fast approaching its zenith. By this stage the Beasties had established a reputation for goofing around and acting up, being more than a little boorish and sexist, and for not really giving a shit. And the band's media coverage subsequently split neatly into three areas, too. There was the "ban this evil filth" angle, the "they're outrageous but they're from nice middle class families, so they're even more despicable because it's all a sham" story, and the "this isn't music!" indignation. A fine early example of all three was provided in *The Daily Star*.

"The Beasties are, most people agree, the most obnoxious group ever," railed journalist Ivor Key, a man clearly no stranger to the concept of hyperbole. "They play the sort of music that parents love to hate," he notes, and, clearly excited by accidentally getting something right, he succinctly analyses that 'Fight For Your Right' is "nothing like their usual material." He then gives full vent to his ignorance and misconceptions about rap music, taking up the sort of establishment *vs* youth culture moral high ground that has been proved to be so spectacularly out of touch every time it's been used since the rock and roll era began.

"There are no melodies, no harmonies, no real singing," he observes, "just a relentless, often obscene flood of depraved words which extol the virtues of raw sex, guns and getting high on alcohol and angel dust. They are loud, talentless and disgusting."

Examining the Beastie live show to add colour and a notion of study to his invective ("They seem to spend much of their time showering each other with beer as they flail and chant to the hammerjack rhythm tracks played by a disc jockey who is up there with them"), Key reads like an amateur anthropologist, always looking in, never understanding or getting close to acknowledging that there's anything here worth more than his contempt. The piece ends with the writer's assertion that the band "have built a reputation on outrage rather than talent" - the notion that you can have a talent for outrage being unthinkable - and stresses a final quote from Mike D to reinforce in his reader's mind that there is nothing in common between either the Beastie Boys and musicians, or rap and music in general: "Next tour we might even play instruments."

This was stock-in-trade tabloid newspaper reporting. Key has looked for what he knows will outrage his readers and gives them gratuitous detail which is designed to titillate as much as to highlight deviant behaviour (the piece is accompanied by a photograph of a woman removing her top while on stage with the band, captioned "DEPRAVED"). It was a piece designed to reconfirm prejudices in order to sell papers. In the tabloid sales war, it would appear, the truth is most certainly the first casualty.

Accompanying Key's piece was a smaller story which quoted the suitably "outraged" Conservative Member of Parliament Peter Bruinvels and outlined his desire to see the group and their records banned from entering Britain. "Their kind of trash is obviously very dangerous," rails the easily offended Tory, who adds "our children will be corrupted by this sort of thing." Bruinvels' fellow Tory MP, Geoffrey Dickens, clearly didn't even wish to concede that the Beasties were human. "I want these diabolical creatures banned from these shores," he told *The News Of The World*. Bruinvels and Dickens belonged to the school of British politicians that felt his or her chances of re-election were best enhanced by being able to provide prospective voters with a bulging file of press clippings to emphasise their high public profile. Consequently, they were always willing to offer an emphatic opinion on any issue and would be quoted frequently in the tabloid press, regardless of the issue or their detailed knowledge of it. They became known as 'rentaquotes', and, satisfyingly, many of them found their seats in Parliament rather more difficult to hang on to than they clearly had imagined. That the Beastie Boys are still with us long after Dickens and Bruinviels have been consigned to history's dustbin is perhaps a small victory.

Underlining their own suss and subtly showing the tabloid pack they had a bit more going on upstairs than they were being given credit for, Yauch laughed off the railings of the Tories as the band briefly stopped off in London on their way to the Montreux festival. "All we're doing is having a bit of fun," he told *The Sun's* Craig MacKenzie. "The problem is we're living in conservative times. With Reagan and Thatcher running the countries, people act like it's a big deal."

"There were debates in parliament about...whether we should be able to bring our 'inflatable' penis, which was actually hydraulic," Diamond recalled to *Q*. "I've always had this visual image of very earnest people in wigs discussing the merits of a hydraulic penis."

There is some truth in the axiom that there's no such thing as bad publicity and, for a band in the Beasties' position, stories like those already printed could do very little harm. *Of course* they're offensive and parents don't understand them: that's what rock and roll's supposed to be about. If you're appealing to the rebel spirit in teenagers you're hardly going to find it a handicap if those teenagers' parents are less than whole-hearted in their praise of your band. Consequently, and in common with the majority of pop acts that find themselves for a time at the centre of the tabloid storm, the Beasties and their representatives decided to play along with the papers and grant interviews and photographs to keep the press coverage ticking over. When the band arrived in Montreux, Switzerland, for an appearance at the city's annual pop festival, where they would perform alongside the legendary likes of Smokey Robinson, the tabloids were foaming at the leash.

"My job with the Beasties was to try and cause as much chaos as possible on the road and build the press story as it went along," John Reid, the band's road manager told *Q* in

1996. "We did deals with a lot of the journalists out there [in Montreux] to keep the press thing moving."

The wheels finally came off, though, when *The Daily Mirror* ran their front page headline story on May 14th. Headlined 'POP IDOLS SNEER AT DYING KIDS', the piece accused the band of mocking crippled and terminally ill children. The story, by Gill Pringle, would prove difficult to live down, regardless of the fact that it wasn't true.

"Gill Pringle had been hanging in Montreux trying to get a story and she had asked Adam Horovitz for a few words," Mike told *Q*. "He blew her off because he didn't have time and because she'd been snubbed she just made up the entire story."

Pringle reported that the band had told a group of young "mainly terminally ill leukaemia sufferers" to "'Go away you fucking cripples'."(The ever-prurient paper replaced the letters following 'f' in the adjective with asterisks.) Pringle further maintained that the group had laughed and sworn at the children and that they were "roughly pushed aside as the three-man cult band rampaged through a plush hotel after a five-hour drinking spree which left a trail of destruction." Her attempts to ask the group to explain their actions met with short shrift: "When the group's Adam Horovitz was asked about the incident he sneered: 'Who cares about a bunch of cripples anyway?'"

"When I read it, I was really pissed off," explained Mike D. "I felt powerless to convince anyone it wasn't true. We didn't sue the paper although we did consider it, it would have been too costly. There was actually a small retraction printed much later but by then the damage had been done. I had to phone my Mom and tell her that I wasn't really a cannibalistic, child-eating mass-murderer."

The band found an unlikely, if temporary, ally in the shape of *The Mirror*'s deadly rival in the battle for circulation, *The Sun*. Previously, on the day Pringle's story had occupied their nemesis' front page, *The Sun* had also been hot on the Beasties' tails, though their story stopped some way short of potential libel. Reporting that the band had got drunk, sworn at reporters and cameramen and that Yauch had had what appeared to be a fight over a groupie with Run DMC's Jam Master Jay, the paper's reporters gleefully described the band's insurrectionary activities. Noting that Yauch was "drunk after knocking back brandy and vodka cocktails called 'Cold Medinas'" ('Cold Medina' would become a catchphrase for Public Enemy's Flavor Flav, and 'Funky Cold Medina' was even later a hit single for Tone Loc, whose producers, the Dust Brothers, worked on the Beasties' second LP - further examples of Beastie slang becoming part of hip-hop's colloquial vocabulary), the paper reported the rapper's comments at a subsequent press conference as though they constituted a threat to the fabric of British society. "We're going to carry on drinking our Cold Medinas, taking drugs and falling on our faces," Yauch is quoted as saying. "If people in Britain don't like it they know what they can do." He further endeared himself to every right-thinking anti-reactionary soul across the globe by suggesting that the appropriate course of action to be taken by the Tory MPs who'd been campaigning to have the group's work permits refused would be for them to "Fuck off".

So it must have been with some heaviness of heart that *The Sun* found themselves running a story supporting the band the following day. While Pringle and *The Mirror* stood by their earlier story, repeating their accusation and supporting it with Pringle's apparent eye-witness claims ("I WAS THERE...I SAW the tears spring into the eyes of two children who asked for their heroes' autographs and whose dreams were shattered,"), *The Sun* found themselves sticking up for the band they'd spent a month assassinating the character of, in order to undermine the authority of their main competitor. Quoting a mother of one of the children ("The Beasties were very kind to the children and happily signed autographs for them," said Pauline Hallam), and pop star Paul Young, a patron of the Dreams Come True charity that had paid for the children to visit the festival, *The Sun*'s piece set out to rubbish Pringle's claims. "OK, so we get drunk, fight and smash up bars," admitted Yauch, in half a sentence vindicating the previous day's *Sun* smear, "but we know where to draw the line. Who the hell would want to upset a bunch of kids who haven't got long to live?"

In a side-bar to *The Sun* story, which reported that the band had gone on yet another late night rampage in Montreux, this time - tsk, tsk - attempting to turn over two parked cars, the Beasties received what would for some time to come be one of the most perceptive analyses of their attitudes and psyches. That this should come from the celebrated topless model and, at that time, putative pop star Samantha Fox is surprising enough. Fox became famous as a "page three girl", a peculiar institution to the British tabloid press: a busty young woman is pictured topless on page three of the paper each day, thus making a mockery of the editorial direction - which always leans towards conservatism and prurience - with the oft-voiced opinion that "it's just a harmless bit of fun." The difference between "harmless" Sam and her ilk and the "diabolical" Beastie Boys stage show, with its topless women and ludicrous giant phallus, is rather difficult to discern. So, for that matter, is the difference between three blokes behaving lewdly and talking about sex and a woman famous for baring her breasts having as her first hit single a song that went "Touch me, I wanna feel your body". Unless, of course, you're a tabloid newspaper employee, or a page three girl. "They are the sort of boys," opined 'sexy Sam', "whose heads used to be stuck down toilets at school." Clearly a kindred spirit.

Sam was still seething when the third British tabloid on the scene, *The Daily Star*, entered the fray. She told their reporter: "They're awful, horrible - just one big turn-off." *The Daily Star* led with the car incident, and two photographs of the band trying to overturn it, and also quoted Larry Blackmon of Cameo, who said "That band is giving pop a bad name." Blackmon, a past associate of the hardly titillation-shy George Clinton, once appeared on *Top Of The Pops* wearing a bright red (and, one presumes, significantly oversized) codpiece, provoking a record number of complaints to the BBC only broken years later by the programme's broadcast of the Prodigy's 'Firestarter' video.

The game, though, was almost up. *The Sun*, exhibiting some of the finer traditions of investigative journalism, had tracked down families and friends of the trio and set out to shed some light on their past. "I could play the outraged parent," explained Yauch's father, Noel, from what the paper described as a "£1 million ten bedroom mansion in Brooklyn", "but I really find the Beastie Boys whole put-on terrifically amusing." Horovitz' father, Israel, whom the paper referred to as "one of America's most respected playwrights" in a manner that gave the mistaken impression their readership gave a shit, supported Noel Yauch. "Don't you think it's fun how much excitement the boys have created?" he asked rhetorically. "They are not irresponsible. Everything about them is on the side of the angels." (A fuller version of this quote, attributed to *Newsday*, appeared in *The Detroit Free Press*: "I'm extremely proud and not at all surprised. They're very anti-drug and pro-get-to-work, and that's on the side of the angels. He has a talent, and a seriousness, and he's having a lot of fun.")

Incredibly, the band had still to set foot in the UK. As if on cue, the tabloid campaign to deny the band work permits for their tour of the UK abruptly stalled. A spokesman for the Home Office, the government department dealing with immigration matters, told *The Daily Mirror* that Douglas Hurd, the Home Secretary, had personally looked at the case but concluded that "it would be an inappropriate use of the immigration laws in this case."

The remaining few days until the band's arrival in Britain passed reasonably quietly. Yet one significant story ran in *The Sun* on the day the band landed in the UK. With a typical scaremonger's flair, Garry Bushell tried to stir a racial subtext into what the press had already decided would be the inevitable violence. Bushell had championed the extremely suspect right wing Oi! skinhead post-punk movement when writing for music weekly *Sounds*, and his new job at *The Sun* seemed to afford him many more opportunities to stir up similar tensions. His story, which was never substantiated and never repeated (except by himself), quoted an un-named source described only as "an insider" who claimed that in "troubled" Brixton, where the Academy would host the first two shows of the Run DMC/Beasties tour, "black gangs are giving out leaflets with the slogan 'No Whites Allowed'. They think the Beastie Boys are getting rich from black music and they don't want a load of white kids at the show." Residents of the area saw no such leaflets, and, despite rather than because of a massive police presence, the two gigs passed off without incident. That, of course, didn't stop Bushell from pursuing his own agenda. Here's what he wrote about attending the first Brixton gig: "A leering dreadlocked thug held a Stanley knife to my throat and told me: 'If you want trouble tonight, you're gonna get it.' Student trendies recoiled in terror as Rastas and soccer yobs rubbed shoulders with political nutters in Brixton, south London. Tension was running high from the start, after black extremists had circulated race-hate leaflets warning white fans to keep clear. Throughout the show...belligerent black kids tried to pick fights with white fans. They pushed and shouted insults."

Walking to the Academy in Brixton for the first of those two shows on May 23rd was indeed an un-nerving experience, but for very different reasons than those given by Bushell. The venue is situated (literally) a stone's throw from the area's police station, and although concerts there are no rarity, the atmosphere on the night was charged and volatile. Rows of police on horseback stood guard in front of the police station, and while the intent may simply have been to channel concert-goers from the nearby underground station to the venue, to the untrained eye it appeared as though the police were expecting a riot, and were ready for Beastie Boys fans to attempt to storm the police building. Simply getting into the venue from the surrounding streets became something of a nerve-jangling affair: as the band's future British press officer, Anton Brookes, who attended the Brixton shows as a fan, recalled when speaking to *Q* some years later, "The atmosphere was heavy - there were loads of police everywhere and it felt like you were at a football match." That atmosphere inevitably found its way inside the venue: that there was no riot is simply testament to the good-nature of the people attending the shows.

The Beasties, their dancing girls and their hydraulic penis, then, became something of a sideshow. Run DMC, the headliners in everyone's minds but the media and the police, were who the majority had paid to see. And the threat of some sort of trouble probably dulled the occasion for many. While the inevitable edginess surrounding an event held under such circumstances can add a frisson of excitement, to many people the threat of trouble, and their own safety in the event of it, became the over-riding concern.

In what was one of only a handful of pieces written about the band's trip to Britain to see through the surely transparent facade, *The Independent*'s Dave Hill gave his own account of going to the Academy show. "The management of The Academy had sought to cover themselves by a combination of PR and heavyweight security, which, had its implications not been so gloomy, could have been cheerily described as a farce. As teams of bristling bouncers frisked you from head to toe with crackling phallic symbols, there was a leaflet to read, urging patrons to behave for fear of losing future promotions 'of this nature'."

"What the Beasties contrive," Hill continued, "is half low *Animal House* humour and half lumpen role playing. So spectacularly impotent is their libidinal posturing that the offensiveness of having caged go-go dancers on stage comes close to symbolising their comprehensive uselessness to any sane female person. So crass is the sensibility they assume as the springboard for their routine that only the naive could construe them as some sort of ideological vanguard. Few rap punters would be so uncool as to actually *follow* a bunch of loons like that…A persona has been filched and perfected so completely that the line between acting off and really meaning it has become blurred: which just about defines most adolescent boys."

So far, then, there'd been no real trouble (aside from that bloke threatening Garry Bushell). In Liverpool, though, a combination of a self-righteous attitude among people who'd bought tickets after reading Pringle's story in *The Mirror*, and felt that the band needed to be "taught a lesson", conspired with the group's and their management's underestimation of the seriousness of the situation to produce a real riot for the press to gloat over.

Fundamentally, perhaps, overestimating their audience was the band's only mistake. "I think anyone who's smart enough can see the joke in it," Yauch had said while touring the States. "It's an inside joke between the three of us; with our success, the joke has become public property. It's worked its way into best-selling records, but the joke's still ours, so it's OK. People don't credit kids with the intelligence to listen to music and see that it's a joke. Parents get too uptight. The music is for the kids; if the parents don't like it, that's their problem."

In the same way that the south Bronx had become synonymous with urban decay through repeated images of the multiple malaises affecting it in the mid-70s before the birth of hip-hop culture, so in the mid-80s, Liverpool had become intractably linked with the failing fortunes of industrial Britain. Margaret Thatcher's Conservative government had done their best to break the spirit of working class people in Britain, most obviously through the protracted attempt to crush trade unionism through the bitter years of the Miner's strike between 1984 and 1986. During an overlapping period, Liverpool city council was controlled by a Trotskyist organisation, Militant, who provoked a head-on conflict with the government by refusing to stick to what they maintained was an inadequate budget set by the Conservatives with which to run local services. An area already reeling from the loss of almost all its local industry through the ravages of the global economic recession, Liverpool had further to deal with the systematic erosion of local services as the council and the government played out a war of attrition. It was not the sort of place to play if the press had managed to convince elements of somewhat hopeless local young people that your band was a pampered shower of middle-class brats, playing at being from the street, who thought it was a laugh to take the piss out of crippled kids. Given that the date didn't sell out before the worst of the tabloid stories appeared, it seemed inevitable that some sort of problems would arise.

"The Glasgow and Liverpool dates were added after the tabloid stories broke," Diamond explained to *The Detroit Free Press*, "so there were a lot of people who'd come to see the spectacle rather than the band. Liverpool was unbelievable. The bottles started flying 'cos most of the people there just wanted to get drunk and start a fight. We were in a no-win situation. If we didn't go on there'd be a riot for sure and if we went out and asked the crowd to stop throwing shit then we'd really get bombarded. We just decided to give it a shot and see if we could get through."

"Ah, man, Liverpool," Adrock began, recalling that fateful night in a later interview with *NME's* Ted Kessler. "Three songs in and we realised that *all* the audience are singing, but not one of our songs. So we asked our English friend, The Captain, what was going on and he said, 'It's really bad, they're singing football songs.' Then the bottles and cans started flying in from everywhere."

The band attempted to play through the hail of debris. Finding the going decidedly tough, they took a brief respite but came back on-stage with baseball bats and tried to hit things back towards the crowd. By the end of the third song, they gave up all pretence of making it through the set and retired to their tour bus. "Once we were on the bus we thought, 'Thank God it's over,'" Mike D recalled. "'All English people are assholes.'"

Yet it wasn't. On their arrival back in London in the early hours of Sunday 31st, Horovitz was arrested and charged with an alleged assault of a female fan, who claimed to have been hit in the face by a beer can pelted from the stage by the baseball bat-wielding Beastie. "I spent the weekend in the police cells, which was a drag because it was a long weekend," Adrock told Kessler. "I never threw a thing, I was totally innocent." On advice from tour management and the record company, Yauch and Diamond left the country while Horovitz was questioned at Notting Hill police station. "We weren't being disloyal to Adam," Mike D recalled, "but there was nothing we could do for him." "My friends were sharing it with me, in a way," Horovitz said to Kessler. "Do I recognise myself? Think of the time you were the most drunk, hugging the toilet, fucked up and ugly...but happy in a way. Do you recognise that? Me too." Adrock appeared in court on June 1st and was released on bail of £10,000. A court appearance, where the charge of grievous bodily harm to 20-year-old Joanna Marie Clark would be heard, was set for Liverpool Crown Court on July 21st.

Tabloid accounts of the evening in Liverpool were predictably lurid. Most of the reports carried claims from people who heard sectors of the crowd chanting "We tamed the Beasties", *The Daily Star* also quoting Liverpool Royal Court Theatre manager Simon Geddes as saying that a proportion of the audience wanted to give the band "a taste of their own medicine." All laid the blame for the melée squarely at the Beasties' door, with Geddes quoted in *The Sun* in a rather less equivocal frame of mind: "They incited members of the crowd to violence and that is unforgivable. We could have sorted out the troublemakers if the band had simply walked back off the stage when the missile throwing started."

As Horovitz travelled to Japan to meet up with Diamond

and Yauch and continue the band's worldwide tour, he could have been excused more than a little room for wondering just what he'd gotten himself into. Although the memories of those close to events suggest that much of what happened was easily shrugged off, some wounds took time to heal.

Speaking in 1998, Bill Adler recalled that "it seemed to me that they could wear the scorn of the British press easily, they could wear it like a *crown*, but when the kids themselves seemed to pick up the attitude of the press and turn their scorn on the Beasties, once that started that wasn't fun, that wasn't something that they loved, it got dangerous. That Liverpool thing was a very dangerous thing. I do not think that Adrock loved being arrested. I don't think that it was traumatic for him, but it was kinda crazy."

Once out of the UK, events calmed down. "When I toured with them in Europe, they was cool guys, I had fun with them," remembers Run. "Runnin' around, doin' shows, just enjoyin' the success. None o' that (the tabloid bad boy image) was true. They was calm, normal guys. I don't think they cared about none o' that stupid stuff. I don't think they worried about what the press was sayin'. They knew who they were and whatever the press thought was what the press thought."

"They got through it, they came back to America, and the record continued to blow up for another year," Adler explains. "That had virtually no impact on their career - it was just a bad week in England."

A bad week, nevertheless, that marked the end of the band's first fifteen minutes of fame, and was enough to put them off visiting the UK for some five years. As the infinitely more tragic stories of murdered rappers Tupac Shakur and Notorious B.I.G. would later prove, there's a price to be paid for allowing a cultivated public image to obscure reality. The Beastie Boys would never make the same mistake again.

CHAPTER FIVE

"Who do you talk to during the hiatus?"
Mike D, July 1989

The touring rumbled on. And on. And on. By the time they'd been round the USA twice, had visited Europe and Japan, causing ructions and Richter scale-measurable commotions along the way, the Beastie Boys reckoned it was time to relax and spend some of their money. But other people didn't see it the same way.

"After they came off the road, all of these issues came to a head and things unravelled pretty quickly after that," remembers Bill Adler. "It was very complicated, there are a lot of factors at work. A lot of these forces were in play for a while and there was a lot of royaling around during the time that *Licensed To Ill* was blowing up. I think when you have a runaway hit like they did things get crazy anyway, there's a lot of money, a lot of fame, and they really were blazing hot and that's a hard thing to weather even under the best of circumstances."

That these were not the best of circumstances should be self-evident. Stressed out by the demands of such a long tour, and further agitated by the peculiarities of their situation, the band themselves weren't getting on well with one another. A number of divisive factors that had been simmering beneath the surface now had the opportunity to come to the boil. While touring so hard had been stretching the group to somewhere near breaking point, not working would prove to be just as dangerous.

The group splintered after coming off the *Licensed To Ill* world tour. Adrock, who had begun an intense relationship with actress Molly Ringwald, headed off to Los Angeles to pursue a movie career. He starred in a film for director Hugh Hudson: *Lost Angels* found him cast as a middle class youth experimenting with gangs, and despite winning over critics and getting praised at the Cannes film festival, the movie failed to make an impact at the box office. Mike D and MCA, meanwhile, both had other bands they intended to play around with, and while the group always maintained they never ceased to be an entity, confusion reigned as to the Beastie Boys' future.

"There had been a lot of struggle over the Beasties," says Adler. "Basically Rick had been trying, in his own way, and a not very subtle way, to saw off Horovitz - he saw Horovitz as this great creative force - and he wanted to...I mean, I don't know what his plan was, as he was much closer to Adrock, but he ignored Mike D and Yauch, and that had been happening for quite a while and that had caused a lot of friction in the group, going way back to '84."

Speaking in 1989, however, Rubin saw things rather differently. "Before the success I was big friends with Adrock, he spent one summer living in the same dorm as me and we'd hang out together all the time," he told *NME*'s James Brown, who interviewed the producer in his Los Angeles home, "and then when we became successful we'd still hang out but there'd be all these business managers and other people telling the other two I was trying to split the band. It's success, suddenly there's so much pressure being applied to every situation by so many people. Also, people change."

Rubin told Brown that the band had broken up following the end of their extensive period on the road to form individual projects, a claim the Beasties at the time denied, maintaining that they had always been involved in outside groups anyway: "Nobody talks about my separate bands!" complained Adrock to the *NME* scribe. "We've all had separate bands since we were fourteen, my bands being the better separate bands." Rubin also didn't mention another factor cited by Adler: "[Rick] wanted to make movies with them but they fell out over the ownership of the script, he probably wanted more than they felt he deserved." Adler admits that at some nine years distance his recollection is "sketchy."

Nevertheless, Rubin claimed that Yauch in particular had wanted out. "There were all kinds of things going on when they were breaking up, a lot of that was personal stuff between band members. I would get phone calls from different band members saying, 'I don't want to do this anymore, I hate that other guy, I can't picture myself doing this.' CBS asked us for another record, and we told them there was no more Beastie Boys because Yauch had asked Russell to manage his new band, and Horovitz was out here seeing Molly and was going to be a film star and Mike had his own band as well." (This story dovetails with the rumour that Simmons had his own ideas about a solo career for Yauch: generally regarded as the most conventionally skilled of the three rappers, the fact that he already had the one-off 'Drum Machine' single behind him supported stories that claimed the Def Jam boss had earlier earmarked him for solo success).

Adler continues the story: "Adrock at the time was tight with Molly Ringwald and however he felt about the group, he tended..." He pauses to refresh his memory. "He'd get very involved with the women he was with - she was his shelter from the storm. At the end of a lot of gigs, he would fly off and spend the weekend with her, wherever she was, and then he'd burn back and continue the tour. They were conducting a very serious affair at the time...I don't know if they ever talked of getting married but...probably...it was all a little vague, but that was just one more thing that was happening at the time."

"CBS said we couldn't have any more money because we weren't delivering what our contract required," Rubin claimed. "So we explained this to the Beastie Boys and they just said 'Fuck you'."

Adler's recollections differ somewhat. "They were spending money kinda wildly. All I know is that when they finally came off the tours...they had been working like pigs, the Far East,

Japan, and when they finally took a breath and said 'Pay us our royalties!', Russ, for his own reasons, didn't seem to want to pay them straight away. He was sure that if he paid them they would all fly off in different directions and that would be the end of the group. He decided for managerial reasons not to pay them then. I don't know to what extent that holds water but that was what he was saying. Their attitude was 'Fuck you, we earned the money, give us the money!' I'm not sure exactly what happened, but probably when Russ wouldn't pay them, they decided that they would find someone who would. They went out on to the open market, even though they had a contract with Def Jam, because they felt that Def Jam were in breach of that contract by allegedly not paying them royalties."

Lawyers acting on behalf of the band wrote to both Def Jam and Rush in the autumn of 1987 to inform Simmons in both his capacities that the Beastie Boys felt that the label was acting in breach of their contract. Def Jam and Columbia responded by filing a lawsuit that alleged that it was the band who had broken the contract by failing to begin recording a follow-up to *Licensed To Ill*. Speaking to *Rolling Stone*'s Fred Goodman in 1989, Simmons claimed that by withholding the band's royalties he was simply trying to push them into beginning a new record. "All I said I needed was a commitment. 'Just reaffirm your deal.'"

According to *Rolling Stone*'s report, the band's lawyers felt there was more to Simmons' claim than met the eye. The piece quotes the group's attorney, Robert Weiner, as being doubtful over Def Jam's ability to pay the reported $2 million in question. "I think there are serious questions as to whether Def Jam could pay. Due to that inability, they created excuses why they shouldn't pay. We don't believe Def Jam could have paid the Beastie Boys under any circumstances."

"There's a discrepancy because some people want records to come out and we really don't do records like other bands, we don't follow those schedules that other people do," Mike D told Brown in *NME*. "You can't just sit us down and do it, it took us nearly two years to write the first album. What do you think about what happened? You go on tour in England and everybody says horrible things about you, you play in a riot, and then you go on and tour for four more months than you really want to. It's beyond drudgery, it gets to the point where it's worse than the guy who sits on the bridge in the toll booth, you're doing that for months. And after that you don't get paid for what you've done for the whole year. We're not really interested in talking about what happened, it sucks. When we made the deal with Def Jam we made the mistake of it not being just based on business but based on a friendship that we thought we had."

And of the state of that friendship during the protracted legal parrying, Mike was blunt. He told Goodman at *Rolling Stone*: "I'd like to say I have no animosity but that would be a lie. How can you not dislike someone who stole from you?" This would still be the Beastie line in 1994 when they recorded *Ill Communication*, their fourth album. In 'B-Boys Makin' With The Freak Freak' they use the following metaphorical allegation to suggest the expansiveness of their sound: "Got fat bass lines like Russell Simmons steals money."

The legal situation still unresolved, the band decided to plough ahead regardless and instructed their lawyers to put out feelers for a new record deal. Capitol won a reputedly fierce bidding war, securing the Beasties for an undisclosed sum that music industry insiders - in particular, sources who claimed they'd been involved in the bidding - reckoned to be worth between two and three million dollars to the group. *Rolling Stone* reported that the label's president, David Berman, reckoned his company "had the legal right to sign the Beastie Boys, or we wouldn't have done it."

"The Beastie Boys were gone before I was gone from Def Jam," Rubin explained to *NME*, already ensconced at his new label, then called Def American, which would subsequently be forced by the threat of legal action to change its name to American Recordings. "I don't think I've ever been told why they left. When I was leaving they were at the point where they were breaking up and as far as I knew they were never going to be making any more records."

Appearing resigned to losing the group, and seemingly determined to make their departure as awkward as possible, Simmons informed the press of his intention to follow up any new Beasties album with his own record of vocal out-takes applied to new backing tracks that he was to title *Whitehouse*. Tapes of some of these mis-matched demos do exist, and although the record was scheduled to be released some six weeks after the Beasties' second album, *Paul's Boutique*, it would never be made commercially available. Tracks that are reputed to have been included on *Whitehouse* include a version of The Beatles' 'I'm Down', which Michael Jackson, who owns the copyright to John Lennon and Paul McCartney's songs, had refused to allow them to release alternate takes of tracks from *Licensed To Ill* with slightly different lyrics and a repetitive nursery rhyme-like piece with ludicrously over-the-top crack references called 'The Scenario'. When asked about *Whitehouse* Simmons was unrepentant, the Beasties derisive.

"You can say it's dirty but I think they owe me. That's eight gold records I've got to replace," Simmons told *Rolling Stone*. "We're gonna make a record with Russell rapping over fucking chickens barking," sneered Yauch to *The Face*. "You wanna know where the [*Whitehouse*] album is?" Mike asked *Melody Maker*'s Ted Mico. "It's up here in Russell's head. That's all it's ever been. The tragedy is that Russell is someone who really likes music, but he never got someone in to organise things so he didn't have to play by the rules of this bullshit industry. They still owe us a lot of money, but we don't know when or how much we're going to receive. There's no point in winning a million dollars' worth of claim tickets."

"The thing about all these manipulator guys like Russell and Malcolm McLaren," Mike told James Brown in the *NME* feature, "is they take what essentially happened by accident and they take credit for it. Switching record companies really made us learn. All of a sudden we had to do a crash course in record companies and in six months we just about learned everything. And what pissed me off is that record companies don't seem to listen."

Mike would later put this knowledge to work when setting up his own record company: indeed, semi-jocular stories circulated that he'd even been interviewed for a senior job at Capitol. No one paid it much heed at the time, but the soon-to-be entrepreneur was clearly learning as he went along.

The Def Jam situation wasn't the only series of legal ructions the band had to get through between becoming stars and making their second album. There was still the matter of Adrock's unfinished business in a Liverpool courtroom. To nobody's great surprise, and to substantially smaller notices in Britain's press, the Beastie was cleared on 11th November 1987 of assaulting Joanne Clarke, who had alleged the actual bodily harm. Duncan Birrell, prosecuting, had called on three witnesses who had confirmed that the rapper had pitched the can "low and hard" at Clarke, while Horovitz's lawyer, Sir David Napley, contended that the only issue was whether or not the rapper had thrown the can. Horovitz maintained he had only waved a baseball bat and hadn't thrown anything, and an off-duty police officer who'd been at the gig was among witnesses who backed up his story, contradicting those who had appeared for the prosecution. Magistrate Norman Wooton found that "on the evidence before me this defendant can be given an entirely clean name." Adrock's father, Israel, was in court with his son, and the two were visibly relieved the trial was over. "I am not happy," the rapper told the press afterwards. "I am just sorry she got hurt. I will be returning to Liverpool but I can't say when. The press make us out to be raving maniacs and at Liverpool we seem to have attracted a football crowd ready to fight." Clarke's solicitor, Rex Makin, indicated that his client would be pursuing a civil case for damages. "In America they talk in telephone numbers, not like the English courts," he told *The Times*. Despite the result of the case, though, several people who attended the concert that were spoken to during the researching of this book seemed to back Clarke's allegations unprompted, though a twelve year old memory cannot perhaps be entirely trusted. Makin no longer holds files on the case, but he recalls that Clarke apparently won eventual damages in Britain, though it is unclear whether these came from Horovitz, his or the band's insurers, the venue or elsewhere.

It was after their departure from Britain that another story germinated, one that, more than any other, has passed into Beastie Boys legend. As part of the hip-hop parody of *Licensed To Ill*, Michael Diamond had taken to wearing an outsized Volkswagen radiator grille medallion on a chain around his neck. During the period when the group made the album, a number of rappers and hip-hop fans took to sporting gold chains and expensive jewellry; some also drove flashy cars. No one is entirely certain when the two got put together, but certainly by the time of Eric B & Rakim's 1986-released *Paid In Full* album, people had started wearing chains with Mercedes Benz insignias hanging off them. Mike's visual joke was therefore an attempt, once again, to take the piss out of the genre and his concocted Mike D persona. VW was never the coolest make of car in the world, and its angular logo hanging from a chain round some fool's neck was hardly the last word in style: yet the joke caught on, largely with an oblivious public who probably took most of what the band did and said at face value. Almost immediately, Volkswagen radiator grilles around Britain were separated forcibly from their badges while their owners slept; the car manufacturer, inundated with requests from peeved motorists, sent out thousands of replacements free of charge. They even offered the same service to Beasties fans, but that was, evidently, where notions of naffness began to enter the picture. Stealing the uncool emblem was cool; applying for one by mail order sucked. Beavis and Butthead would have felt right at home in England

MCA and friend, early '87

The Beasties in Montreaux (crippled children allegedly out of shot)

Adrock: "It was this big!"

Mike D - VW owners' most hated figure, '87

The boys say "wassup?" to the British tabloid press

Horovitz gets stoopid, London '87

Yauch and Diamond at the London Marquee, '92

Mike D rocks the Rough Trade shop, London '94

"Beastie: phone home!"

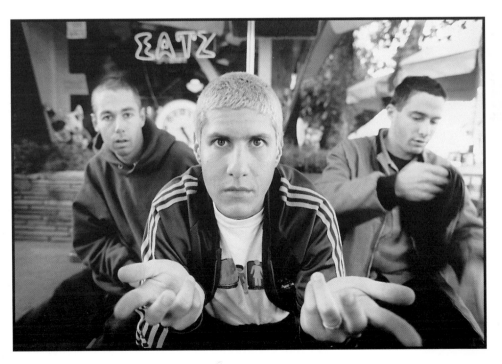

"So what, so what, so whatcha want?' Mike D orders eatz, '94

Yauch: it's the pits - Tibetan Freedom concert

Horovitz, Diamond and Yauch check your head

in the late 1980s.

Despite the laughs and the frankly ludicrous behaviour of a significant number of their fans, though, this was not a good time to be a Beastie Boy. With so much gnawing away at their resolve, this period could have seen the disintegration of the band. Yet, like the greatest of artists, out of adversity they would craft another masterpiece.

CHAPTER SIX

"The man upstairs - I hope that he cares,
If I had a penny for my thoughts I'd be a millionaire..."
'Shadrach', from *Paul's Boutique*

By the time the Beastie Boys second album, *Paul's Boutique*, was released, the band probably felt they were due a break from the great gamesmaster in the sky. After all the work and crap they'd been through, seemingly not getting paid was the final insult. So, as if to prove their worth to anyone who'd ever doubted or questioned them, they moved from New York to Los Angeles, its newly emerging rival as hip-hop's capital city. Living in a blaxploitation movie fantasy pad, spending money like it was going out of fashion and consuming and digesting more music than ever before, they returned with a record brimming with creativity, wit and intelligence.

Paul's Boutique marked the opening of a new phase in the Beasties' career more emphatically than any of the band's fans could have envisaged, and was very much more than a logical follow-up to *Licensed To Ill*. Indeed, in almost every respect, the record is so dissimilar to its predecessor as to appear to be the work of a different band. The acerbic humour, free-form allusions and popular culture references were intact, but *Paul's Boutique* was an entirely different proposition to the cross-market potential of the debut album.

The record was apparently titled after a men's clothing shop in Brooklyn, pictured on the cover, but the truth is rather more complex. The sleeve was lavish, particularly in a limited edition vinyl pressing which arrived in an eight-panel folding cover that reproduced a 360° photograph of the site of the store. But the street corner pictured - the junction of Ludlow and Rivington Streets - is in fact in on the Lower East Side in

Manhattan, not Brooklyn, and the sign that claims the shop is the fabled Paul's Boutique is actually hanging from a different store altogether (Lee's Sportswear). What now seems likely is that the band had decided to name the LP after the real Paul's Boutique, only for the shop to go out of business before the cover was shot. Ultimately, though, the deception is unimportant. The intention of the title would seem to have been to metaphorically suggest something of the browsing around and mixing and matching of musical source material that the record indulged in: certainly, *Paul's Boutique* finds the Beasties adopting a thrift store shopping mentality to their seemingly haphazard collection of beats and rhymes.

The LP arrived after months of speculation and showcased a band not so much pushing the envelope of hip-hop's by then often formulaic production techniques as tearing the package out of the postman's hands, ripping it into pieces and burning it. In cahoots with Los Angeles production team the Dust Brothers, the Beasties managed to create a record that felt free and uninhibited in its approach to sampling from diverse source material, in the process creating a sparkling backdrop across which they ladled lyrics that revelled in their own convolution.

The first track proper of the record, 'Shake Your Rump', sets what might be considered the album's template: beats are introduced and dumped with astonishing quickness, rhythms are explored, augmented and embellished only for them to be snatched out of the mix abruptly, ruptures and discontinuities are as important as linear flow is to conventional western music. [For a detailed and quite brilliant discussion of rupture and repetition in hip-hop music, see '"All Aboard the Night Train": Flow, Layering and Rupture in Post-industrial New York', in Tricia Rose's book *Black Noise: Rap Music and Black Culture in Contemporary America*]. Yet after some investigation, what appears to be a chaotic and free-form assemblage of random beats reveals a fairly straightforward verse-chorus structure, complicated only by the frequency with which musical elements are changed.

Paul's Boutique is defined by its resistance to definition: just when you think you know what's coming next, the record zips off at another unexpected tangent, never to return. This doesn't just apply to the music, where bluegrass banjos wrestle with funk loops, psychedelia and the sound of people playing ping-pong, but extends to the almost free-associative lyrical approach, too. Yet in both music and lyrics, the one unifying factor seems to be the Beastie Boys' reliance on the hip-hop attitude: *Paul's Boutique*, though artfully constructed and relentlessly complex, sounds like it was slung together freestyle. It is b-boy to the bone.

The opening lyrics of the album are "Well I can rock a house party at the drop of a hat/I beat a biter down with an aluminum bat." Typically battle-rhyme rock hard, typically Beastie Boy jocular cool. That they're delivered brashly, arrogantly, self-confidently by Mike D and Adrock simply emphasises that the Beasties had developed their own consummate take on rap's fundamentals. As stylists they are unique, but as hip-hoppers they are more than mere curiosities. Go through the record and you'll trawl up swathes of lyrical flotsam and jetsam, all evidence of the unique personalities behind the record, but all at the same time testament to the Beastie Boys' singularly creative and ultimately very reverent approach to hip-hop culture. This is a record that *demands* its creators be respected as emcees. "I feel that I need competition to better myself constantly," Mike told one journalist as the album was being released. "I have an over-riding need to be a better emcee at all times." The proof? Try 'The Sounds Of Science', where the three voices trade syllables of the line "Expanding the horizons and expanding the parameters" before Yauch patiently declaims, "Expanding the rhymes of sucker MC amateurs."

There are lyrics that ponder the process of writing lyrics - an emcee staple - and battle rhymes ready to go head-to-head with the best the rest can muster. Musings on the nature of the group's creativity rub shoulders with drop-dead funny asides that rubbish public figures and elevate cheesy TV celebrities to the level of statesmen and world leaders. When MCA talks about being the gelatinous material inside the lava lamp of his brain, or the three voices simultaneously compare their lyrical and mental flows to an oil projector, you're aware of the group demonstrating the fluidity of their style while recalling the psychedelic era the music often evokes. In 'What Comes Around' another apt metaphor for Beastie creativity is employed - one their earlier detractors would presumably find helpful: "Reach into my mind for the rhymes that I'm seeking/Like a garbage bag full, overflowing, now it's leaking." And in 'Shadrach' - a tale derived from the Biblical story of Shadrach, Mesach and Abednego - the group make an (admittedly esoteric) attempt at a mythologised auto-biography. "One has to admit they lived a somewhat hectic life," Horovitz told Ted Mico in *Melody Maker*, speaking of the trio who refused to worship a golden image and got thrown into a pit of fire, which they seemed to thrive in. "What happened was," Yauch elaborated, "they didn't get paid by their former record company so they went to Capitol. The story has a good ending."

'Johnny Ryall' attracted much attention from reviewers for its sympathetic depiction of a homeless man the Beasties knew from around the way in New York. For some reason, the band told *Request*, Ryall thought Mike was called Frankie. "I'd feel bad correcting him," Mike told journalist Keith Moerer, "but he definitely has a lot of stories about not getting paid. So Johnny has become our main adviser." This, and a few lyrical passages that warned listeners away from certain class A substances, were held up as evidence of a maturing by the band: a patronising notion dismissed by Mike, with a certain degree of irony, as being "a complete misinterpretation".

Yet there are other, less often noticed examples of a burgeoning social conscience to be found. The Beasties frequently attack racism ('Looking Down The Barrel Of A Gun' attests that "Racism is schism on the serious tip", while the otherwise largely bonkers 'Egg Man' notes that if "You make the mistake and judge a man by his race/You go through life with egg on your face"), but that's hardly a revelation. What is rather more surprising, from a band so supposedly asinine, are the passages that energetically and imaginatively lambaste politicians and the police. Adrock accuses the boys in blue of manufacturing crack in 'The Sounds Of Science', reinforcing a little-voiced but street-popular ghetto conspiracy theory. The three emcees go to work, in 'Car Thief', on wife beaters and tax cheaters, before returning to the earlier theme: "Buy me cheeba from the cop down the street." That commentators and fans overlooked such lyrics, though, is at least partly the band's fault: rarely, if ever, have such talented lyricists played down the seriousness of their work. Even though much of the record is approaching the flippant, there's plenty here for even the most furrowed of brow to delve into. Yet even the biography circulated to journalists with advance copies of the LP by the band's new label went out of its way to discourage any kind of earnest consideration.

Paul's Boutique bows out with a twelve minute multi-part track called 'B-Boy Bouillabaisse', a selection of snippets of New York life loosely bound together by their shared brevity. It forms a sort of final summary of what the record's all about, as Mike explained to *The Face*: "In making the bouillabaisse you might have fishermen from all around the village bringing in different fish. You might have a coupla farmers bringing in some tomatoes just to *thicken* the stew." It's as good a description of the creation and form of the album as you're going to get.

So *why* does it sound like this? Is it an attempt by the Beasties to redeem themselves in the eyes of people who didn't get off on their stupid image by returning with some self-consciously clever music? Certainly not, if the album's recurring lyrical themes - sex, food, drinking, acting like a prat and a curious and frankly baffling obsession with the word "rope" - are anything to go by. If anything, the Beasties do their best to steer intellectuals away by making the album as offensive as they feel they want to. There is too much offhand and casual sexism for the politically correct listener to stomach (Adrock's lines in '3-Minute Rule' provide a good example, a tirade against money obsessed women culminating with the line, "You're a dog on a leash like a pig in a pen"). Obviously, as musicians interested in being at the cutting edge of their genre, both the band and the producers would have been concerned with making a record that didn't slavishly adhere to any previously established rules, but even that in itself doesn't fully explain what's going on here.

Two key factors seem to have influenced the direction of *Paul's Boutique*. Firstly, the band were clearly energised by their relationship with the Dust Brothers, in whom they found kindred spirits with a deep love for, and awareness of, hip-hop history. And this in itself is the second key element: *Paul's Boutique*, like 1989's other great hip-hop *meisterwerk*, De La Soul's *3 Feet High And Rising*, goes back to the roots of hip-hop music in an attempt to find the inspiration needed to move the art form forward.

A chance meeting in Los Angeles in February 1988 led to the Beasties and the Dust Brothers working together. Mike Simpson and John King, aka EZ Mike and King Gizmo, had earned an ever-growing reputation on LA's still relatively underground rap scene as radio jocks and some-time producers. By the time of *Paul's Boutique*, they and cohort Matt Dike, who ran the LA-based rap label Delicious Vinyl (and had met the Beasties when he'd launched the label in New York), had scored major success behind the boards with their work with gravel-throated LA rapper Tone Loc. Interestingly, the notion that the Beasties had gone looking for the Dust Brothers after their success with Tone Loc rankled with the band, as Mike D told *Kerrang!*: "When we came out to LA to work with him [Dike] it was strange to hear the reactions... 'Matt who?'

Now people look at it and say, 'Oh, last time Rubin, this time Dike's the big name in rap'. Which is, of course, misinformed and stupid, but what can you do?"

Dike, the third Dust Brother, was DJ-ing at a party in Los Angeles that the Beasties attended: Horovitz was working on a film and hanging out with his then girlfriend, actress Molly Ringwald, and Yauch and Diamond, disillusioned after their falling out with Def Jam, were along for the ride. At the party, Dike played some tracks the Dust Brothers had planned to use for their own album, and the Beasties were hooked. Approaches were made that ended up with the two trios getting together in the studio within a matter of days.

"We were excited to work with them," Simpson told *Bay Area Music Magazine*'s Nancy Whalen six years later. "We had been fans for a while, and had played their earlier singles and subsequent album on our show. We Fed-Ex'ed a tape to them in NYC, and waited anxiously for a response. Two weeks later, they called and said, 'We're getting out of our deal at Def Jam, and we want to do a record with you guys for Capitol. Book studio time for tomorrow, we want to start working.'"

A combination of factors meant that recording took an incredible sixteen months to complete. The major factor seems to have been the Beasties' concentration on lyrics: certainly the dense and multi-layered writing bears this out. But the relatively arcane technology at the Dust Brothers' disposal surely contributed. The samples, which sometimes number up to twenty per track, were recorded one at a time on an Emax machine that limited the producers to twelve seconds per sample, and the songs were assembled laboriously, piece by piece. "We filled 24-track tapes with loops and scratches running all the way through, and arranged the songs using Neve and GML automation in the finest studios in LA," Simpson told Whalen. "The people who worked at the studios thought we were crazy at the time, 'cause they had never seen anybody make songs that way. At that time, the production on hip-hop records was quite minimal. We were looking to produce edgier, more emotional records that would sound a little different each time you heard them."

"We did songs then put them aside," Simpson told British rap magazine *Hip-Hop Connection*. "Months later we came back and worked on them again. I would say that the sound on the album is definitely a combination of six spirits who brought all of that to life. It wouldn't have been the same without any one of us. The Beasties hung out with us and fourteen months later we had a finished album."

"It's a six-way thing," Mike affirmed when speaking to *Melody Maker*'s Ted Mico in LA immediately prior to the album's release. "It was very much a democracy. Democracy may not work for America, but it seems to work for us."

"We like things that people recognise but don't know who or what it is," Simpson told Whalen, attempting to contextualise the record's eclecticism. "All the ideas came to us in visions. We'll be listening to something and we'll have a few tracks made and then, all of a sudden, somebody will remember a Tito Puente record or a Sammy Davis Junior record. We were mixing shit like Black Oak Arkansas with Sly & The Family Stone, or Alice Cooper with the Crash Crew. To get just the right sound, we used a blue bong, high quality indica buds, hash, hash oil, freebase, red wine, cigarettes, LSD, coffee and whippets."

Jocular it may be, but Simpson's reference to psychedelic drugs seems apt. Although it may be an over-used comparison, it's still valid to assert that, in many ways, *Paul's Boutique* was, in 1989, pretty much as near as hip-hop had got to emulating The Beatles' classic *Sgt. Pepper's Lonely Hearts Club Band* album. Both are loosely conceptualised, both offer testimony to the mind-expanding properties of certain proscribed chemical substances, and both became touchstones in the histories of their respective musics, landmark albums cited as the epitome of what their genres were capable of. Also, as noted by several reviewers, *Paul's Boutique* is opened and closed by 'To All The Girls' and a reprise in the same way *Sgt.*

Pepper's is book-ended by the title track. And both albums are essentially collaborative efforts between the bands and their producers (George Martin's arrangements and orchestrations constitute as concrete an involvement in, and as significant a contribution to, the sound and form of *Sgt. Pepper's* as the Dust Brothers work does to *Paul's Boutique*). Entering wholeheartedly into the Beastie spirit, *NME*'s James Brown poured scorn on this comparison as he attempted to explain *Paul's Boutique*s obsession with food: "Someone mentioned *Sgt. Pepper's Lonely Hearts Club Band*. Colonel Saunders Hungry Chicken Club Gang more like."

The Beatles, bizarrely, appear frequently on *Paul's Boutique*. 'The Sounds Of Science' uses loops from 'When I'm Sixty Four' and 'Sgt. Pepper's Lonely Hearts Club Band (Reprise)' and utilises scratches from 'The End' (from the *Abbey Road* LP). In the closing 'B-Boy Bouillabaisse', the Beasties use the same approach - stitch a few different songs together for no readily apparent reason - as The Beatles did at the close of *Abbey Road*. Like *Abbey Road*, too, *Paul's Boutique* is unconventional in its structure: there are few breaks between songs, and the tracks themselves often take outrageous twists and turns and display dizzying variations in pace, style and tone. Even the slightly mysterious and contrived story behind the sleeve has a Beatles-esque ring to it. Yet Mike Simpson played down any suggestion that the Beatles samples were there for anything other than aesthetic reasons. He told *Hip-Hop Connection* that "The Beatles do show up on the album, not because we're giant Beatles fans but because they did have a wealth of incredible breaks on their records."

Yet the claims implicit in a comparison with so exalted an album as *Sgt. Pepper's...* is one borne out by *Paul's Boutique*. It simply *is* that good. "What turns *Paul's Boutique* into a killer is the breadth and depth of madness, depravity, hilarity and plain stupidity in the nerd word dissin' an' rhymin'," observed *NME*'s Roger Morton as he awarded the record eight out of ten. "It's like someone gaffa-taped your face to a late night US

TV screen, switched out the lights, and sat there flipping channels in time to an in-built rap rhythm."

Morton's colleagues were, in the main, united in their praise of the album, and as the immersion of hip-hop music and culture into the mainstream had continued during the band's hiatus, many writers arrived at *Paul's Boutique* better equipped to understand the Beasties and their context. "Their greatness lies in inveigling their way to the heart of hip-hop, inflating and exaggerating its mannerisms like they were blowing up so many condoms - the bragging, the pilfering, the sexism, the street swagger," opined *Melody Maker*'s David Stubbs sagely. "That they are able to do this three years on and sound this fresh, this crucial, this confounding, seems miraculous." Over at *Rolling Stone*, David Handelman described the record as "meticulously constructed", but acknowledged that the spot-the-source aspect of listening to the album was only a small part of a larger picture: "the musical 'steals' effected by the Boys and the Dust Brothers... are much more complicated than the first album's, changing speeds, inverting or abstracting themes until they're new. If you can recognise them, fine, but they stand on their own; it's no more thievery than Led Zep's borrowing from Muddy Waters." "They're still unlistenable and uncivilised in the best and most attractive sense of the words," beamed an effervescent Charles Shaar Murray in Q. "*Paul's Boutique* is a record for kids to play in their rooms loud enough to disrupt their parents' Dire Straits-accompanied dinner party, or for nervous home-owners to sling on the stereo while they're out in order to convince prospective burglars that they're not only at home but throwing a party."

Even pop-oriented magazines and the heavyweight news media acclaimed the record. *Time* magazine ran a brief story applauding the range of cultural references dropped by the band, and linking their peppering of the lyrics with dropped names to the way the music itself is constructed out of fragments of other people's original material. "They not only purloin sounds but ransack culture and drop almost enough names to rival Andy Warhol's diaries," maintained Emily Mitchell, who also acknowledged that the group had "raised [sampling] to an art form". The magazine's review of the album was similarly unstinting in its praise: "At the risk of sounding ridiculous, let us assert right off the bat that *Paul's Boutique* is as important a record in 1989 as Dylan's *Blonde On Blonde* was in 1966," David Hiltbrand told his readers. "[The Beasties] place themselves right on the threshold of art... guess what? These wiseacres just delivered the most daring, clever record of the year."

"*Paul's Boutique* resonates with that energetic sense of well-being that enables youth to cock a snook at every last piece of advice offered by its elders and supposedly betters," opined *The Times'* David Sinclair. (Another writer to link the record to the wider aspects of hip-hop culture, Sinclair made the perceptive analogy that the trio's voices "scatter their bratspeak lyrics across the rhythm tracks like kids spraying graffiti over the bumps of a brick wall".) Developing the same theme for a very different readership, Miranda Sawyer told the readers of *Smash Hits* that the album is "all most jolly and certain to annoy your Mum and Dad if you turn it up loud enough."

While the majority salivated over *Paul's Boutique*, certain mid-market newspapers and some sections of the rap media formed a curious alliance against the album. "Heroism is not normally a quality associated with the rather sedentary role of rock critic," sneered *The Daily Mail's* Marcus Berkmann, "but listening to this album twice through is undoubtedly the most courageous task I have ever attempted. This is - and let's not be equivocal about this - the single most tedious album by a supposedly 'major' act that I have ever heard." Observing that "where De La Soul take the piss out of hip-hop and put a whole lot back, these Beasties take the piss out of hip-hop and keep it!" *Hip-Hop Connection* found common ground with the non-rap-literate when remarking that "none of the tracks have any song structure to speak of." Although *Hip-Hop Connection*'s principal problem with the record was a perceived lack of loyalty to hip-hop culture, the assertion that this was a confusing and somehow non-musical record is one that recurs in many of the negative reviews of the band throughout their career.

While it's fair to say that the riff-laden guitar-led extravaganzas of the *Licensed To Ill* era were conspicuous by their absence (the metal mayhem of 'Looking Down The Barrel Of A Gun' notwithstanding), complaining about a lack of songs on *Paul's Boutique* is as off-beam an observation as carping that Picasso put too many noses on his cubist portraits. Yup, the Spanish master probably realised there were more than the requisite number of facial appendages in some of his images. And the Beasties too would be aware that what they were doing on their new LP went against the grain of much of the music they were pitched against. Yet both were innovators concerned more with moving their art forms forward than appealing to those who only wanted to deal with repetitious revisions of the past. On *Paul's Boutique,* the Beastie Boys and the Dust Brothers crafted a forward-looking, experimental music rooted in the liberating form of hip-hop and the concept of sampling, but paying little heed to the expectations of either the band's existing audience or the whims of a capricious music marketplace. In this regard they succeeded where many before them had failed. The question everyone seemed to be too shy to ask, though, was - why *them*?

It's no secret. It's there in the grooves of the vinyl, hidden deep inside the lavish limited edition eight panel fold-out sleeve, behind Ricky Powell's portrait of the band submerged in a swimming pool, covered in psychedelic goo (cosmic slop?), sandwiched up against the microscopic print of the lyric sheet and the woodcut images of exotic fish. Scratch beneath the disorienting surface of *Paul's Boutique* and you find a record steeped in the heritage of hip-hop culture, a record that, despite its modernity, is deeply rooted in a vibrant tradition. If it was just a musical Frankenstein's monster, beats and samples stitched together by some deluded if technically brilliant dabblers, the record would fall to pieces before your ears. But because it's organic, grafted from a living, breathing idiom and filled with life and vitality, it draws you in, beguiles and seduces you, and keeps growing.

Listen to 'Shake Your Rump' carefully and hear how it's pieced together, and what from. Those old school rappers from the time of the music's genesis used to each get individualised beats when they got their turn on the mic, and the Beasties are no different. The music just shifts quicker because they don't wait until the end of the verse to swap vocal duties. And where do all those snatches and scratches come from? Where else but the ever-expanding library of hip-hop, from the old school to the very new. 'Shake Your Rump' features large chunks of classic early '80s hip-hop from the Sugarhill label - the Funky Four Plus One More's 'It's The Joint' and the Sugarhill Gang's '8th Wonder' (the sample used, "ooh-ah, got you all in check", would be appropriated and amended to form the chorus and title of a massive hit single in 1995 by Busta Rhymes). The latter's 'Sugarhill Groove' is sampled in 'Shadrach', as is a different portion of 'It's The Joint' (tellingly, the words used are "being very proud to be an emcee"). Public Enemy's 'You're Gonna Get Yours' and 'Bring The Noise' feature in 'Egg Man' while a sample of KRS-ONE from Boogie Down Productions' 'My Philosophy' crops up in '59 Chrystie St.', the first part of 'B-Boy Bouillabaisse'. The heavy rhythms in the guitar-dominated 'Looking Down The Barrel Of A Gun' are from 'Last Bongo In Belgium' by the Incredible Bongo Band - a track that appears on the same album as 'Apache', one of the original breakbeats that Kool Herc played at his early '70s Bronx parties, and is therefore as close to the essence of hip-hop as you can get.

Paul's Boutique, then, is a traditional hip-hop album made at a time when the first wave of sampler-liberated productions had begun to wane. After the monumental successes of '87 and

'88 (two albums each by Public Enemy, Boogie Down Productions and Eric B & Rakim, one from Ultramagnetic MCs and a slew of incredible 12″ singles), hip-hop had become co-opted into the musical mainstream. Up to this point the majority of the experimentation that was key to the music's growth and success had been in the hands of artists and sympathetic independent labels, who realised that they could make money by servicing the growing audience with material that remained true to the culture's core values. Once major labels and multinational corporations got heavily involved, though, the music became much more conservative: with a mass market being the only one that interested the companies, only rap music with potential mass appeal - that is, rap for people who didn't like rap, since they constituted the majority - was invested in. So the higher profile rap releases usually weren't anywhere near the best. The Beasties, who had shown that hip-hop could succeed outside New York and across the world, had proved that it could make a connection from Los Angeles to Laos, had inadvertently and accidentally played a part in ensuring that the music they loved was stagnating. By taking hip-hop music back to its roots, *Paul's Boutique* can be seen as the Beastie Boys' hip-hop first aid kit: their attempt to provide an ailing music with an adrenalised shot in the arm. Or, as Yauch told Ted Mico, "I would say that if this album is saying anything, it's saying that we love music. That is, indeed, the central statement in my eyes."

A laudable, praiseworthy and exhilarating record that's simultaneously progressive, experimental and rewards repeated listening by opening up to inquiring ears, *Paul's Boutique* should have become one of the acknowledged all-time classic albums. Instead, *Spin* magazine would later describe the record as one of the most under-rated LPs ever; 'Hey Ladies' barely scraped the Top 40, and the album sales were similarly disappointing. That this happened is probably down to two key factors: firstly, the unyielding nature of *Paul's Boutique*'s experimentation is off-putting to the casual listener, thus making across-the-board acceptance unlikely. The second, and probably more problematic reason, though, was that the Beastie Boys suffered from a case of poor timing. After such a protracted genesis, *Paul's Boutique* was beaten to the record shops by De La Soul's *3 Feet High And Rising*. A superficially very similar album, De La's debut is almost as good as *Paul's Boutique* but, because it came out first, the Long Island trio stole much of the Beasties' thunder.

Similarly concerned with re-invigorating hip-hop from within, *3 Feet High...* - released by Tommy Boy, the independent label that Columbia had toyed with signing before they plumped for Def Jam in 1986 - shares much common ground with *Paul's Boutique*. For starters, there's a shared sense of the piss-take about each album: while *Licensed To Ill* perhaps better represents the Beasties' tongue-in-cheek approach to rap conventions, their second album also seeks to undermine clichéd rap posturing, albeit more subtly. De La Soul's pacifist, disarmament-symbol-encrusted "D.A.I.S.Y. Age" image was contrived in no small part as a rejoinder to the newly emerging gangsta rap genre and hip-hop's depressing preoccupation with gunplay and wearying machismo. Both records display a rampant eclecticism, both rely on the interplay of a vocal trio, both are the work of a group alongside a gifted and visionary producer (De La Soul worked with the hitherto unheralded Prince Paul, a member of the Russell Simmons-managed, Tommy Boy signed group Stetsasonic); both appropriate elements of '60s psychedelic culture, both can be termed "concept albums" (*3 Feet* is linked by skits from a non-existent game show) and both have a strong sense of hip-hop history. Check De La's 'The Magic Number': a melodic loop gives the track an accessible, almost pop feel, but the main part of the song is based on the classic DJ record 'Lesson 3' by Double D & Steinski, from the *History Of Hip-Hop* EP (three tracks sketching the evolution of the music, each one described as a 'lesson', and numbered).

Both records also, by a quite mind-boggling coincidence, sample country & western legend Johnny Cash. On 'Hello Brooklyn' from 'B-Boy Bouillabaisse', the Beasties use a segment of the Man In Black from the classic *Live At Folsom Prison* album ("Just to watch him die" was Cash's character's reason for shooting a man in Reno in the song 'Folsom Prison Blues'). Meanwhile, over in De La Soul's world, the very title of *3 Feet High And Rising* comes from a sample of Cash's '5 Feet High And Rising', included in 'The Magic Number'.

It is impossible to mention Johnny Cash in a Beastie Boys context without noting that his re-emergence and subsequent re-adoption as a fashionable musical icon followed him signing to the American Recordings label and releasing, in 1995, an album (also titled *American Recordings*) produced by the label's boss - one Rick Rubin. Los Angeles rapper Ice-T told *NME* in 1993 about how he believed country & western and hip-hop were closely linked, and used the Johnny Cash line sampled in 'Hey Brooklyn' as evidence to support his claims. "To me rap has a real strong parallel to any traditional music, but especially country & western. You might laugh, but think about it! They sing about their neighbourhood, they wear jeans and hats when they go to the Grammys and they sell millions of records but nobody knows who buys 'em. The way we sing about our urban environment, they sing about their rural environment. I mean, listen to Johnny Cash! He sings, 'I shot a man in Reno, just to watch him die'. That's a Geto Boys lyric! Bushwick Bill would do that same thing! So there's a lot of similarities, we just do it to different beats."

With the points of comparison almost converging like this, it's little wonder that those spellbound by De La's album might have found the Beasties' record lacking. Yet such a point of view assumes that the Beasties and the Dust Brothers were aware of what De La Soul and Prince Paul were up to: given the fact that they were recording at opposite ends of the US, and knowing the time frame over which *Paul's Boutique* was constructed, this is impossible. Nevertheless, the notion seemed hard to shake, and the Beasties were the losers both commercially and in terms of how the records would be perceived by posterity. *3 Feet High And Rising* substantially outsold *Paul's Boutique*, and won almost every music magazine critic's end-of-year poll going. The Beastie Boys' masterpiece, in the grand scheme of things, didn't matter - because it came out a few weeks too late. Bugger.

CHAPTER SEVEN

"People how you doing? There's a new day dawning..."
Opening lines from 'Jimmy James',
first track on *Check Your Head*

Success and failure are relative concepts, and the Beastie Boys now found themselves with plenty of time to ponder them. Between *Paul's Boutqiue* and the next LP, the band would disappear from public view for the better part of three years. They were, at least, phlegmatic. As Adam Yauch would later point out, many bands would have been ecstatic with what were, in the light of *Licensed To Ill*'s phenomenal quantities, considered to be *Paul's Boutique*'s poor sales. "Most musicians I grew up playing music with would probably shoot me if I ever complained about selling 800,000 records. It's definitely not a number to sneeze at," he would say in *Star Tribune* in 1992. But the world-conquering, multi-million-selling enormity of *Licensed To Ill* had altered the grounds of perception of what constituted a hit or a miss. Based on their expectations, the sales of *Paul's Boutique* suggested to Capitol that they'd made a particularly poor investment.

The Beastie Boys had compounded Capitol's problems, though it was really more a case of the label not realising until it was too late when to call a halt to the threesome's spendthrift spree. The problems had begun before *Paul's Boutique* had even been finished. The sessions had taken place at a series of expensive studios across Los Angeles, and the band, still not fully relocated to the extent of having set up home in the city, had been put up in a lavish private house. Filled with the owners' kitsch '70s clothes, the house - likened by Mike D to a "total *Dolemite* fantasy world" - came complete with a bedroom that had a window into a swimming pool, where band friend and de facto photo-documenter of all things Beastie, Ricky Powell, would shoot what was to become the inner sleeve portrait photograph for the album. The owner had made the mistake of leaving her impressive garment collection in place while the band stayed: the temptation these items provided was always going to be too strong to resist. The house was decorated with a gold letter 'G' on the front door: the Beasties, never likely to miss the chance to indulge in innuendo, rechristened it The G-Spot. Money, much to the delight of a band still to enjoy the fruits of the success of their previous album, was no object.

Capitol should have been anxious to ensure the band stuck to a strict regime and delivered a record on a budget that made some sort of sense. Blinded, though, by the profits another *Licensed To Ill* would make, and confusing the group's laissez-faire attitude with a method for making hit records, the label clearly didn't keep close enough tabs on the band's progress or the money they were spending. The fact that a record as amazing as *Paul's Boutique* got made at all is incredible enough: but when you realise its creators spent most of the time they were supposed to be making it playing ping-pong and wearing womens' clothing, the record takes on an extra, more miraculous air.

"For the first time we had complete creative and financial freedom," Mike D told *Select*'s Adam Higginbotham. "When we made *Licensed To Ill*, we'd be like going into this bummy studio at two in the morning. And then all of a sudden we were here [in LA], going into these fancy studios where you pay like $1500 a day. And we'd just go in there and play ping-pong. Seriously. We'd play ping-pong, we'd order up air-hockey tables. We were completely retarded. I mean, it was really ridiculous… and in a lot of ways, a lot of fun." (To say that the ping-pong table added nothing to the album would, however, be incorrect. You can hear the band playing during of 'The Sounds Of Science'.)

"And then with the artwork on the album and everything,"

Horovitz added, "we pushed them to the limit. We just pushed them to the absolute limit you could possibly push a record label. And all of this with them having the expectation that they were going to sell a lot of records!"

Mike butts back in: "And then, and *then* - the *best fuckin' part*, after we'd spent all this money playing ping-pong, the record did not even sell anything!"

The launch party for the LP was held on the roof of the label's headquarters. A Dixieland jazz band played a selection of top tunes while barnstormer aeroplanes wrote the band's name in massive dusty letters in the sky. Capitol's famous office building in Hollywood - designed to look like a stack of singles on an old-fashioned record player - was supplemented by a 50-foot Beastie Boys flag ("People just don't understand how beautiful something like that is," Diamond complained to Higginbotham). A week before the release of the album, the A&R executive who'd signed the band left for a holiday and never came back. At least one person had sussed that the advance the band had been paid was in addition to the skyrocketing recording costs and the daft promotional expenses, and that the resulting record was likely to go over the heads of the hoped-for mass audience.

It was a hoot while it lasted, but when the label went cold on the band, refusing to spend money promoting a record they felt was never going to recoup the original investment, the Beasties were left to their own devices. The critically lauded but relatively poor-selling LP was dormant on the shelves; touring was impossible as the record company coffers had been bled dry (though the band would later insinuate that behind-the-scenes manoeuvering had also prevented any tour from taking place). A crisis of confidence at this point would probably have finished the band off: instead, they underwent a transformation more complete than they'd made between *Licensed* and *Paul's Boutique*.

Taking a step back from the almost confrontational experimentalism of the last album and rethinking their role, the Beasties made a series of key decisions. Firstly, they surrounded themselves with a protective ring of close friends who, largely, would remain their working partners to the present day. Then they made the move to Los Angeles permanent, and built a studio in Atwater Village they would name - presumably in reference to the *Paul's Boutique* living accommodation - G-Son. And they returned to their roots as traditional instrumentalists, bringing guitars, bass and drums that were played by themselves rather than sampled into the frame for the first time since the B-side of 1984's 'Rock Hard'.

G-Son was their investment, the base they built with the last remains of Capitol's *Paul's Boutique* advance, and it would become something of a fortress of solitude as they metamorphosed from three geeks with an apparently shattered career into the ultra-credible post-slacker generation supermen they would soon become. Capitol let them get on with it - after what was to them the disaster of *Paul's Boutique*, they seemed not to care whether the Beasties ever made another album, and as long as they were in their social club/recording facility they were at least out of harm's way.

The room in G-Son in which live instruments can be recorded has a couple of other purposes: it doubles as a wooden-floored basketball court and houses half-pipe skate ramps. Visitors have mentioned the atmosphere in G-Son being more akin to a youth club than a recording studio, and it's this relaxed ambience that would permeate the group's next two albums. That they were extremely contented is a given. "If we had a fantasy when we started out, say like when we did that hardcore record 'Polly Wog Stew' - if we'd had someone say, 'Well, what would you guys really want?', we probably would have said 'Well, just like a studio where we could go play music and hang out all the time,' and that's what we had," Mike affirmed to Dave Larsen in *The Montreal Gazette*.

Mario Caldato Jr, the engineer who'd worked on *Paul's Boutique*, had become a trusted friend and would remain a creative part of the band indefinitely. Studio engineering is a tricky business, relying on an understanding of the musicians as much as on technical aptitude: working out how to achieve a sound that's just right for the people you're working with when the back of the reverb unit looks like an accident in a spaghetti factory is a peculiarly complex talent. In hip-hop styles of production, the engineer can often be more of a translator of ideas onto tape than a producer on a more conventional rock recording. For the Beasties to have found someone as happy dealing with live instruments as samplers and DATs was a huge bonus. Caldato had become involved with the band in typically inauspicious circumstances: when the Beasties had managed to assist in the disintegration of a PA system three bars into the first song of a set at Matt Dike's Los Angeles club Power Tools, Caldato suggested to the Dust Brother that it was high time he hired a professional sound man. He was on the payroll within a week and soon began working on *Paul's Boutique*.

When, one evening, Mike crashed his car into the wooden gatepost at the G-Spot, Caldato's high school friend and ivory-tickler extraordinaire, 'Keyboard Money' Mark Ramos Nishita, got the call to come and repair it. Nishita's carpentry skills were up to par (the band later serenaded his woodworking achievements on 'Finger Lickin' Good': "Keyboard Money Mark you know he's not having it/Just give him some wood and he'll build you a cabinet"), and he got the job of constructing G-Son. By this time, the fact that he was a keyboard-specialised multi-instrumentalist into the bargain had permeated the Beasties' collective consciousness and had earned him a place in their band. The group also secured a management deal with John Silva and Danny Goldberg of the LA-based Gold Mountain company, whose clients at the time included the band who were in the process of becoming the biggest rock act on the face of the planet, Nirvana. Long-time live DJ Hurricane, who'd replaced Rick Rubin's short-lived successor, Dr. Dre of Def Jam group Original

Concept, remained part of the clique. (This Dre is not to be confused with the former member of NWA and producer of Snoop Doggy Dogg's debut LP: the Beastie-affiliated Dre went on to find fame as half of the Ed Lover and Dr. Dre team that presented *Yo! MTV Raps* and the breakfast show on the influential New York hip-hop station Hot 97. The duo also starred as cops in the rap comedy film *Who's The Man?*) Thus, along with long-time friends like Ricky Powell, the Beastie Boys had effectively constructed a ring of, if not steel, at least protective personalities and like-minded spirits they felt they could rely on. Their move west had made it possible, though they resisted notions of this being a peculiarly Californian way of living. "LA enabled us to create our own world," Mike D explained in *DJ Times*. "We were able to build our studio...by having our own little world and studio we can create whenever we want to create, at the pace we want to create, however we want to create. That's given us that feel - not just being in LA. It would've been very difficult to have that feeling in New York." Sounds comfortable, doesn't it? It was from within such a potentially productive and almost totally self-contained environment that the group made their musical swerve.

The reasons why the next album saw Beasties take a step away from hip-hop can only partly be explained by the muted public reaction to *Paul's Boutique*. At least as big a part of the reason why they incorporated live instruments, smoky funk jam sessions and hardcore thrashings on their next record was to distance themselves from the worst excesses of what seemed to be a declining musical form. While the Beasties and De La Soul had done much to suggest new possibilities for hip-hop beyond the limiting confines of a handful of over-used drum breaks and gratuitously violent and misogynist lyrics, the music as a whole seemed lost and in need of some new impetus. The rise of gangsta rap, cemented though not invented by the unprecedented success and impact of LA group Niggas With Attitude (NWA), had overtaken the genre.

Pockets of resistance to the overwhelming deluge of so-called "reality rhymes" could be found: Public Enemy's third album, 1990's *Fear Of A Black Planet*, continued their examination of racism and reaction in America, and KRS-ONE continued to plough his increasingly solitary humanist furrow; Rakim still occasionally dropped gems of poetical insight and groups like EPMD, Long Island natives with a string of hit albums behind them, were using their success to open doors for talented newcomers they'd discovered and nurtured like Redman, K-Solo and Das EFX. Gang Starr, too, a DJ/emcee duo who'd made their first demos by post (DJ Premier lived in Houston, and sent tapes to rapper Guru in Philadelphia before the duo relocated to New York) had helped forge the jazz-rap sound, sampling jazz musicians and recasting the role of the freestyle emcee as an improvisational jazz instrumentalist; fellow travellers like A Tribe Called Quest and The Pharcyde were bringing the sounds and skills to a different audience. But rap music had become subsumed into the mainstream, divorced from its roots as part of a multi-faceted culture and stranded alone as merely another choice offered to the bloated music consumer. What had made hip-hop culture fresh, exciting and innovative had been replaced by record company marketing budgets, and profit/loss margins were dictating the future of the music. NWA's success meant that, in the predictably lowest-common-denominator mindset of the record business, violent rhymes and hard beats were all that was required. Independent labels struggled to gain any ground, rap innovators were overlooked in favour of whatever flavour of the month sound was selling at the time, and the music was undergoing a period of stagnation the like of which it had never previously experienced.

One huge exception to this rule was Cypress Hill. The LA trio made gangsta rap records with a dusty, almost New York feel, and lead rapper B-Real's nasal voice set the group apart from the majority of gunslinging emcee goons. Cypress are clearly a group stylistically in debt to the Beastie Boys, as

B-Real's voice and elements of DJ Muggs' production bear out, although one key difference between the groups is testament to the fact that they had learned an important lesson from the Beasties, too: over the course of Cypress Hill's three LPs, they avoid the pointless rap fixation with talking slack about women. Because of this, and with the help of some well-planned PR focusing on their support for NORML, the group that sought to change the laws on the use of cannabis, Cypress Hill managed to become practically the only gangsta rap act to have any currency with the 'alternative' music audience. The Beasties were early supporters of the band, and when Yauch and Diamond made an impromptu appearance behind the decks at the London club Listen With Mother early in 1992, they had to be almost physically restrained by the regular DJs (Chris King and the author) from playing Cypress Hill's first album in its entirety.

So the Beastie Boys, inspired initially to become rappers by the limitless possibilities the form seemed to offer as much as by the sound of the music, found again that the best way to move forward was to take a step sideways. The move they made with their third album, to be titled *Check Your Head*, seemed to have been towards alternative rock, but in actual fact they were continuing to mine hip-hop's experimental seam. "People who are making hip-hop records definitely understand where we're coming from because they're used to hearing funky instrumental shit," Mike D told *Rolling Stone* journalist Alan Light as the third album was about to be released. "People who only listen to hip-hop in hip-hop form, it might be a little hard for them to hear at first." Speaking to *The Daily News of Los Angeles*, the rapper/drummer was even more forthright. "People ask us if we're still a hip-hop group. To me it's about bringing hip-hop into a new direction. That's always what hip-hop has been about - innovating. People would do something totally off the wall, in their own style. Then another record comes along and it's a new school. That's what hip-hop is about."

By picking up their instruments again the band rediscovered something of the fun to be had in messing around with different musics, and their limited skills didn't seem to present the same obstacles as they had when their music had been concentrated into a single genre. "The stuff we were listening to and sampling on *Paul's Boutique*, stuff like The Meters and Jazz Crusader, made us think we could set up some instruments and reproduce their funky stuff that we could then sample," Mike later explained to *NME*'s Ted Kessler. "Not that we could ever play that well. Ultimately, we set out to plagiarise this stuff but weren't able to. So it became totally our own sound through sheer incompetence." The freedom and enjoyment the group found in making *Check Your Head* pours out of every groove, and this - coupled with the disdain they show for any notions of generic constraint or musicianly propriety - probably explains why it's such a revered album among other musicians. Oasis' Noel Gallagher has spoken of how the record was practically glued to the band's tour bus stereo for months at a time, and his is far from the only band to feel so enamoured of the record. 'Check Your Head', crucially, feels like the sort of album you'd want to make if *you* were in a band - free of all inhibitions and glorying in nothing so much as its own sense of liberation.

"The whole thing with being a fan of music and buying records is that you're constantly coming across grooves or records that are gonna change your life," Mike would later explain to Aidin Vaziri. "That's the cool thing about music, I'm never going to run out of discovering those records and those records are never going to stop coming out. There's always going to be some group that comes out that changes everything, or there's going to be some group or some group of records that I discover that I didn't know about before that's going to be everything for me also. So it's two-fold, it's like that's going to change my life and it's going to change what I do. I'm going to find little things within that that's going to alter the kind of music that I make." Diamond elaborated on this point to Owen: "When you sample the type of music we do," he said, "you come to respect the incredible musicianship that went into the original. And you want to be able to play like that."

The Beasties' wide range of listening is more than reflected in *Check Your Head* - it provides the record with its primary driving force. Formally, the album, like *Licensed To Ill*, has three basic types of track. Hip-hop, funk and thrash-punk-metal might seem mutually exclusive, but part of the Beasties' genius is in the way they manage not only to allow such different musical textures to co-exist on a single album, but to also effectively let the musics bleed into one another. Just when you think you've got *Check Your Head* nailed down, it's off in a new direction again.

The biggest single difference to the band's previous records is in the reliance on grooves. As opposed to *Licensed To Ill*, with its clattering drum patterns and snatches of riffs, or *Paul's Boutique*'s ever-changing loops, *Check Your Head*'s songs are more organic, self-contained affairs (like the Beastie Boys themselves). That's not to say that when the mood takes them the band don't allow the tracks to cut loose and change - 'Finger Lickin' Good' is constructed in a very similar way to many of the tracks on both *Paul's Boutique* and their 1998 album *Hello Nasty*, with samples (including one from Johnny Hammond's 'Breakout' that Eric B & Rakim used on 1993's 'Casualties Of War') appearing in the mix for a few bars only to be abruptly snatched away - but even in such instances there's an overlaid funky feel, usually from the live instruments, that makes it feel more natural and less a patchwork. It's called funk.

"When you really hear the funk, and it's really on, then that's everything," Mike D explained Michael Jarret in *Pulse!* magazine. "The problem is, the word is so misused, misapplied right now in terms of music, that's it's almost hard to keep the meaning. Adam was talking to this guy about the song 'The Payback' by James Brown. And the guy was trying to say that the guitar was playing nothing. But see, I figure, well, if the guitar is playing nothing, then that means the entire band is playing nothing. But, then, that's the best playing ever on, like, any song. And they're all playing nothing. That's the best shit. To be able to do that, that's the funk. Unfortunately, people confuse the funk with a lot more superfluous musical activity."

"The bottom line with a lot of bands that 'funk' is being applied to is that they don't really listen to funky and aren't versed in funky," he told *Rolling Stone*'s Alan Light. "Like, you know, Gordon Lightfoot." By the time they finished *Check Your Head* the Beastie Boys were, as the funky president himself, George Clinton, would have put it, 'Knee Deep' in the funk.

Recording for *Check Your Head* began in 1989 and the final 50-odd minute LP was condensed from over 100 hours of tapes. The initial notion was that it would be an instrumental album. "We wanted to make it like a breakbeats record," Mike told Frank Owen. "The same way as when you sample you take the best bit of a song, we wanted each song to contain the best bits from our jam sessions."

Inevitably, a quest to reproduce the finest jazz/funk grooves they were listening to would be doomed to failure because of the band's technical limitations. The Beasties weren't after slavish copies, though. "There's no way we'd ever think we could compete with the jazz session guys," Mike D said to *The Daily News* of LA. "I look up to [jazz drummer] Bernie Purdie, but I can't compete with him. The goal is just to play grooves." Horovitz elaborated on what they'd been trying to achieve: "Every song came out differently. Lots of times we had songs done in rehearsal, and we'd go into the studio and try to improve it. But after we restructured it, we would end up going back to the original. The feeling was the thing, not laying down some perfect performance." The best gauge of Yauch's opinion on this is to be found at the beginning of 'Pass The Mic': "If you can feel what I'm feeling then it's a musical masterpiece," he rasps characteristically, "but if you can hear what I'm dealing with then that's cool at least." (He had his bass heroes, too, though. "I've definitely played along with my fair share of Meters records, and I love War," he said in *Orlando Sentinel Tribune*. "It's hard not to for me - I've been doing that ever since I was little. I guess when I was like thirteen and got my first set of headphones and was really listening to different instruments, I got really into bass. I was listening to a lot of Bob Marley back then, bugging out on [Wailers bassist] Family Man.") A good example of the technique can be found by comparing the bass line in 'Jimmy James' to that of 'For The Love Of Money' by The O-Jays, a staple hip-hop breakbeat sample. The Beasties sound like they've jammed around with elements of the O-Jays b-line but adapted it to their own song in a way they might not have been able to do with a sample. Plus, their way is even funkier.

Such a free-form way of working inevitably meant that no real schedule was stuck to. And while the recording process took only a fraction of the three years they were out of the spotlight, deadlines were never really something the Beastie Boys were very good at. "We just messed around a lot," Yauch admitted to *The Orlando Sentinel Tribune*. "We kept playing around with the music and stuff, slowly putting things into place until they were done. We'd actually planned - hoped - on finishing a lot sooner. We kept making deadlines for ourselves and kept missing 'em. It goes back to school - we were definitely constantly absent and late with our term papers and asking for extensions."

The debate about whether the record was hip-hop enough or not raged around the band as they made numerous media appearances following the record's release. "Everyone's got their two cents," MCA told writer Gary Graff. "There were definitely people saying, 'You guys should play, man,' and others who were saying 'Nah, don't do it. Just keep rhyming.' Back when we were a hardcore band and we started rhyming, we had people telling us not to do that, too. You're always going to get some of that. Change is inevitable, and so is growth, but I guess there are people who just want you to stay the same way forever. But we refuse." This refusal produced a quite brilliant album.

Check Your Head's surface details and its multiplicity of musical styles often obscure a key part of its appeal: there are some great *songs* on it. 'Jimmy James', 'Pass The Mic' and 'So What'cha Want' are among their better raps, 'Lighten Up' and 'Groove Holmes' - their tribute to jazz/funk keyboardist Richard Groove Holmes - the equal of any of the plethora of reissued porn movie instrumentals the band's cool factor helped to make fashionable again, and even a ludicrous hardcore punk version of Sly Stone's 'Time For Livin'' works. A brief interlude featuring Brooklyn rapper Biz Markie (whose 'Pickin' Boogers' - a paean to the delights of sticking your finger up your nose - showed that juvenile humour in hip-hop wasn't the preserve of the Beasties as early as 1985) and '70s rock legend Ted Nugent, called 'The Biz Vs. The Nuge', sits well on such a schizophrenic album. Fittingly, considering the band's metaphorical allusions made on *Paul's Boutique* to their music being like a big pot of fish stew, 'The Biz Vs The Nuge' has a food story associated with its creation. "They managed to both be at our studio jamming with each other," Yauch told writer Perry Gentleman. "That was pretty wild. But the high point was actually when Ted Nugent decided to cook us all dinner, and he cooked up a big bouillabaisse. Biz tasted it and thought it was terrible. He went out and bought himself a bag of candy."

Check Your Head's lyrics are often obscured and mixed low in the music. If they weren't printed on the inside of the gatefold sleeve many would be impenetrable, a problem exacerbated by the band's decision to record using deliberately shoddy microphones. "We rocked a distorted mike effect that has confused a lot of people," Diamond told journalist Dave Larsen. "There's some people who realise how fly it is, but there's some people that just aren't with it. Some people think it was by accident, but really, they don't understand that we tried a bunch of different microphones until we could find mikes that sounded like that." The feel, the groove, the aesthetic is allowed to dominate, even at the expense of what the group have to say. And, partly because of this, *Check Your Head* is the only record they've yet made that seems almost afraid of giving anything away. It's the record's only real limitation - as if the Beasties aren't really sure of themselves enough to let you know what they're on about. Taken in context this might well be the case. After the over-riding lyrical puerility of the first two albums, the Beasties were still finding out who they were and what they wanted to say, discoveries all concluded by the time their fourth album, *Ill Communication*, arrived and addressed these issues. *Check Your Head*, in effect, is a document of the Beastie Boys in a transitional phase as they approach some sort of "maturity", and is all the more fascinating for it. It's certainly the first time they offer anything particularly self-revelatory in their lyrics.

The sarcasm and role-playing of *Licensed To Ill* and the group's associated cartoon personas had enabled them to make a record, tour and promote it without ever dropping any clues about who they were. *Paul's Boutique* preferred to develop the artificial characters than expound on the real ones. *Check Your Head*, finally, offers illustrations of the people behind the music. In this regard, too, it is fundamentally staying true to hip-hop's codes. With gangsta rap's predominance, hip-hop's obsession with documenting street reality became all-consuming. Ironically, of course, reality was the last thing many post-NWA gangsta records purveyed. Once the music industry had realised there was a huge market for tales of grim urban squalor, more rappers than you could shake a machine gun-sized stick at came crawling out of the woodwork proclaiming their gang affiliations and flashing battle scars (Vanilla Ice's infamous attempts to convince the press of a life lived "on the mean streets" by displaying a knife scar on his buttock was merely the tip of a Titanic-sized iceberg). "Keep it real" became the mantra rap artists were supposed to obey, only for the phrase to lose its original meaning: "make it up but make it sound gritty, urban and sensationalistically authentic" would have been much nearer the mark in the vast majority of cases. Though, admittedly, not as catchy.

The Beastie Boys, though, kept it *really* real. In the same way that they made *Check Your Head* into a hip-hop record even though it didn't sound like one, so they ensured the lyrics obeyed the music's new cardinal rule, and at once separated themselves from the sham that many were perpetrating in hip-hop's name. Not only did they speak about themselves for the first time: they told of what was going on in their lives, dealt with their own reality, and offered their opinions on the music they had grown up with. Whereas before they would have turned on "sucker emcees" and pretended to be hard, 'Jimmy James' finds the rappers laying their true attitudes on the line: "Not playin the role, just being who I am," they explain, just in case you weren't sure this time, "And if you try to dis me I couldn't give a damn." Some change.

In 'Pass The Mic', Yauch laments the current state of the art, decrying rappers whose subject matter seemed limited to material acquisitions, and explains something of the journey he and his band mates are undertaking. Adrock wonders "What you gonna say that I don't know already?", debunking the notion he'd spent two albums constructing - that he's a fool - and it's left to Mike D to explain most emphatically what life's like as a Beastie at this point in time: "To tell the truth I am exactly what I want to be". In 'Gratitude' they move on to "It's so free this kind of feeling/It's like life - it's so appealing". Clearly, more so than ever before, being a Beastie Boy was real fun, in no small part because they were free to be who they really were for the first time.

Quite who they were when they met up with *NME*'s James Brown again in March '92 at the Gavin Report Convention in San Francisco is a little unclear, though the real question probably concerns Brown's well-being. In a fabulously over-the-top piece of brain-blasted Gonzo journalism, the writer took his cue from the band and wrote a free-associative piece of fictionalised gibberish that succeeded quite brilliantly in summing them up. Claiming to have spent time in a hotel room with Tim Booth from Manchester indie band James, REM's Michael Stipe and Professor Booty, who isn't even a real person (it's the title of a song on *Check Your Head*), Brown found the band expounding a monetary thesis based on the supply and demand of parrots. "You can sell parrots for money," Adrock apparently told Brown on leaving a pet shop called Polly Mixture. "Just gotta buy them in the right neighbourhood and sell them in the right neighbourhood," expanded Yauch, before Diamond weighed in: "A lot of emcees out there are trying to sell a lot of records and be successful...for me I can always play the game. If the record doesn't do much that's alright, I can move some parrots on the street."

With their new sound, a new album and touring as a live band for the first time, the Beasties were in free-form musical heaven. Able to indulge their hardcore tastes as well as rapping, play their funk jams as easily as they could rock the mic, the band threw themselves into touring with a greater relish than ever before. The freedom their stage show gave them was taken to the limits. "What we got into in Japan was like one of us would make a set list and not tell anybody else or show it to anybody else before we'd go on stage, so that way it would be like a jolt of surprise," Mike D told Dave Larsen. "To me that's always what rap is based on, just constant evolution and constant innovation."

They arrived in the UK in the spring of 1992 for the first time since the '87 Liverpool fiasco. Primarily a trip to enable them to complete a number of press and media appearances, they would also play their final gig on British soil, at London's Marquee rock club, as a straight-ahead rap group. By the time they returned in the summer, as part of a double-headline package with former Black Flag vocalist Henry Rollins and his band, *Check Your Head* had been released and some measure of cool had been reclaimed.

More or less everyone loved the record, but it took time. Some dissenting critical voices were raised and it became clear that the album had come as something of a surprise to many reviewers. *The LA Times* said it sounded like it had been recorded in a single afternoon "with time out for beer". *People Weekly*'s David Hitbrand, who had raved about *Paul's Boutique*, concluded that *Check Your Head* was little more than a necessary response to a number of high-profile sample clearance lawsuits and described the album as "thin, unripe and tame". "Next time guys," he advised, "hire a real band." *Newsday*'s Frank Owen, though, spoke for many when he concluded his *Newsday* piece by noting that "*Check Your Head* will be recognised as an instant rock and rap classic." *Details* said it was the group's "most inspired album to date."

And this time the band had the last laugh. To their label's utter astonishment *Check Your Head* broke the US Top Ten on its release, and although it didn't fare nearly so well in Britain, the group's canonisation as the popes of pop cool seemed imminent. A second taste of mainstream success took the Beasties by surprise. "I'm getting freaked out now that the album is starting to sell a little bit," said Mike D in May. "I'm trying to learn how to be comfortable with that. I would never deny anyone the pleasure of selling a lot of records, but it's strange for us. We're this group that's just totally passionate about music and just playing around, and all of a sudden everybody's into us."

Not quite everyone, though: ironically, but perhaps predictably, the hip-hop audience all but ignored *Check Your Head*. In the context of its time, this seemed reasonably easy to explain: as rap had become more mainstream and picked up support from outside its theoretical constituency, so 'outsiders' to the music seemed to want to influence it. This set up something of a siege mentality among hip-hop fans, who would habitually end up decrying the latest rap-influenced band to emerge to critical acclaim as "the future of hip-hop". Groups like the Disposable Heroes Of Hip-Hoprisy appealed to a media that wanted a politically correct version of Public Enemy espousing socialist beliefs to noisy rhythm tracks, using the undoubted communicative potential of the music to expose social ills and posit solutions. Problem was, bands like Hip-Hoprisy weren't usually any good as rappers. They themselves were a case in point: formed out of the ashes of post-punk rock band The Beatnigs, Hip-Hoprisy's Michael Franti was a charismatic and politically outspoken orator who could sloganeer with the best of them, but it wasn't until he was a couple of albums into his next band, Spearhead, that anyone could consider him to be anywhere near becoming a hip-hop lyricist. The Disposable Heroes, Arrested Development, PM Dawn and their ilk alienated hip-hop fans in inverse proportion to the number of glowing notices they received in the music media, finding themselves dubbed "rap for people who don't like rap" by fans jealous of the coverage these comparatively minor talents would get in favour of the more skilled up-and-coming emcees. It was as if the music was being neutered by ignorance of its qualities. Intolerance bred extremism, and the whole 'alternative rap' issue impacted back on the 'keeping it real' theorising with disastrously negative consequences for the music. Things stopped short of lunacy: it never quite got to the stage where having a progressive attitude towards women or some well-thought-out views on social and political change would see you made a pariah by the hip-hop audience. But it was almost that bad. The situation remained unresolved until, arguably, the emergence of The Fugees in 1994, a group who proved that you could play an acoustic guitar *and* be a skilled emcee at the same time. And they wouldn't have bridged the gap if they were white.

Check Your Head, then, reconfirmed latent anti-white prejudices harboured against the Beastie Boys by some sections of their earlier audience, and, by using instruments, consorting with other musics and distorting their vocals, the Beasties were branded card-carrying alt-rappers. The fact that they were more true to the genre, its requirements and its ethos than many of those the rap audience perceived to be "true", was largely overlooked. Once again, by virtue of being ahead of its time, a Beastie Boys album failed to connect with a huge swathe of its potential audience.

CHAPTER EIGHT

"It's definitely crazy sometimes, but you know - fuck it.
There are 24 hours in a day. I can use most of 'em."
Mike D

The Beastie Boys were growing up. That was *Check Your Head*'s clearest message. They still couldn't resist talking rubbish any time someone pointed a microphone in their general direction - their interviews continued to read as if they'd been scripted by the Marx Brothers' post-punk cousins - but the Beasties' reinvention of themselves hadn't stopped at the music. Both Horovitz and Diamond had got married - the former to actress Ione Skye, the latter to director Tamra Davis - and while it would take the better part of another three years for them to follow up their groundbreaking LP of 1992, the time between would neither be spent realigning themselves to a changing musical landscape nor idled away contemplating their collective navel. It was time for the Beastie Boys, quite literally, to get busy.

The challenges thrown up by the ensuing years provoked very different responses from the three individuals. Adrock - the quintessential front man to date, loud and seemingly egotistical - would take a back seat, making a couple of films (including *Cityscrapes*, a voyeuristic trawl around underground Los Angeles directed by Michael Becker and co-starring Skye) but almost vanishing from public view while his friends became more high-profile. Adam Yauch went on a solo voyage of self-discovery, arriving at some sort of enlightenment and realising it was within his power to initiate positive change in situations he grew to realise he cared about. And Mike D became a businessman - though very much in hip-hop mode.

Before hip-hop, the politics espoused by musicians broke down pretty simply. You were either a socialist idealist, who believed capitalism should be replaced by a more equal distribution of wealth according to need (although you generally stopped short of redistributing your royalty cheques anywhere other than your dealer, off-license and real estate agent); or you didn't give a shit. Rock music is so intrinsically linked to notions of rebellious youth that few of its practitioners have chosen to align themselves with the conservative establishment (dishonourable exceptions include proto-electro popster Gary Numan - whose support for the British Tory party at the height of their unpopularity helped send his career, like one of the light aircraft he famously had trouble flying, into a terminal nosedive - and Eric Clapton, who infamously lent support to the crypto-fascist ravings of the worryingly unhinged extreme right wing British politician Enoch Powell). But hip-hop music began to address these unsatisfactory and generally unhelpful positions and tried to find ways of making sense of the reality the music's makers found themselves in. To the dismay of hard-line socialists, who often seemed to feel that hip-hop should of necessity line up against capitalism's divide-and-conquer tactics, rap's leading thinkers looked for ways to make capitalism work for themselves and their constituencies. Dreamy idealism was replaced with a practical pragmatism wholly in keeping with most rappers' obsession of dealing with reality rather than fiction. It is into this context that the Beastie Boys' creation of a cottage industry business empire must be placed.

On their *Apocalypse '91: The Enemy Strikes Black* album, Public Enemy included a track called 'Shut 'Em Down'. PE's Chuck D - a respected thinker, even among those who disagreed with most of what he thought - examined the way large (and predominantly white) corporations invested heavily in advertising and marketing their products in black communities, with the net result that the money earned by black people was immediately being handed over to white multinationals. Targeting in particular sportswear manufacturers and - more directly on the track 'One Million Bottlebags' - the brewing industry, Chuck called for the black community to be more selective in their consumption, and urged people to try to buy from black-owned businesses to help keep some measure of economic control over their longer term destiny. "I like Nike, but wait a minute," he rapped, "the neighbourhood supports, so put some money in it." While his invective was ineffective in directly changing the way large companies functioned in their dealings with black communities, he'd succeeded in sparking a semi-mainstream debate about black economic self-sufficiency. The effects of his attitudes would have a considerable reverberation.

Chuck put some of his money where his mouth was and set up a clothing company called Rapp Style. Advertising their products on flyers included in Public Enemy records, the company was little more than a standard band merchandising operation, but Chuck had shown the way. The years immediately following 'Shut 'Em Down' would see the dominant fashion among hip-hop artists become their contribution to the community that spawned them: as well as keeping it real, rappers now had to give something back to where they came from.

Naughty By Nature, a trio from New Jersey, scored a massive pop hit in 1991 with 'O.P.P.'. A salacious take on the age-old American tradition of cheating songs (blues and country are full of them), 'O.P.P.' succeeded formally because of its easily recognisable sampling of the Jackson Five's 'A.B.C.' and lead rapper Treach's gloriously bubbling flow, and the song's title (which is given a multitude of suggestive meanings, each beginning with "other people's...", though the group only actually state that the other 'p' stands for "property" during the record) became the street catchphrase of the summer. Inspired, in part, by seeing unlicensed merchandise bearing the three letters, the band and their management company, run by successful female rapper Queen

Latifah, set up the Naughty Gear Company to manufacture and distribute their merchandise. The group's logo - their name written as if in crayon with the outline of a baseball bat underneath - was distinctive and street-cool, and their shirts, hats and even jeans sold in huge quantities. But by setting up their own operation and staffing it with friends from their neighbourhood, Naughty By Nature had taken Chuck D's maxims and put them into action. Anyone with a hit record or two can call up a t-shirt company to manufacture and sell their merchandise: but this was a turning point. Within two years NBN had opened a retail outlet for their clothing range in New Jersey, again staffed by friends and people from their East Orange hometown who might well have remained unemployed without the group's intervention.

It didn't stop there. On the west coast a rapper called Paris found his 1992 album, *Sleeping With The Enemy*, was too controversial for the label he was signed to, Tommy Boy, to distribute (the track 'Bush Killer', an assassination fantasy involving the rapper and the then US president, was deemed too much of a hot potato following the commercially damaging controversy that had surrounded the track 'Cop Killer' by Ice-T's metal band, Body Count). Securing a nationwide independent distribution deal and playing the anti-censorship card to a largely sympathetic media, he released the album on his own label, staffed entirely by people he knew from his Oakland, California hometown, and used the record's considerable sales to facilitate the signing and recording of new talent and the expansion of the business.

The emergence of the Wu-Tang Clan in 1993 was low key, but their systematic overhauling of the way record companies did business with rappers led to a reorganisation of how groups were signed and what they constituted. The Wu-Tang Clan's members, though signed to RCA subsidiary Loud Records as a group, were contractually free to sign solo deals with other labels: that the group members would guest on each other's releases was never in much doubt, so effectively they were free to over-run the rap industry like, in their own parlance, a swarm of killer bees. The Clan owned and operated their own management company, again staffed by friends and acolytes from their Staten Island district. Producer and musical master Rza set up a production company that enabled him to make money separately from the group and nurture a clutch of new production talent, and the inevitable clothing line - again emblazoned with the group's unmistakable winged logo - would have no less than four shops across the US by the time the group released their second LP in 1997.

What was happening here was a change in attitudes and perceptions to the prevailing socio-economic conditions that was little short of revolutionary. Just as rap music had invigorated fans, blurring the boundaries between bystanders and participants and encouraging everyone to unlock their inner potential and become musicians, now the rap industry was showing a new generation that it was possible to take firm, real control of your own destiny and that of the people around you. In the commercial civil war, hip-hop had declared economic independence, and it was no surprise to find the Beastie Boys right there in the thick of the battle.

G-Son provided the group with a base to record, but there was other space in the building they decided to turn to good use. The notion of running their own label had long been on the agenda, and by the time *Check Your Head* was released the dream had been made reality, at least as far as adding a name and a logo to the record sleeve and label. And where better to run your label from than your studio-cum-club house?

Grand Royal was named after a phrase the band's collaborator and friend Biz Markie had been habitually using during his time at G-Son working on the album. If he heard or saw something he thought merited particular praise, Biz would declare that it was "Grand Royal - guaranteed fresh". The band thought it would be a cool name for a record label and stuck with it.

Before long the first non-Beasties Grand Royal release, by original Beasties member Kate Schellenbach's new group, Luscious Jackson, wound its way onto the shelves. The LJ connection was part of what tipped the scales and finally got the label started. "It was always something we always said we were gonna do, and finally I guess it was a combination of old friends of ours [who] are in Luscious Jackson giving us a demo tape, which usually we expect to just kinda cringe and be in an uncomfortable position with friends of ours and being like 'Oh, I wasn't really into it'... but here was a case where someone gave us a demo tape and all of a sudden it became our favourite thing to listen to in the tour bus," Mike explained to *Swill*'s Bruce Wheeler. "So we were like, fuck it, we're in a position now where we can put this out, people will listen to what we have to say, so let's do our friends a favour and get this out."

From humble beginnings and relatively low-key ambitions, Grand Royal would eventually build a roster that included Sean Lennon, son of deceased former Beatle John and Yoko Ono, Scottish indie-electro eccentrics Bis, various projects involving members of New York avant-noise blues testifiers the Jon Spencer Blues Explosion, Beastie DJ Hurricane and a succession of other spin-offs the band were involved in to varying degrees. Interviewed in 1992 in *Lies, Lies, Lies*, Mike D listed some of the label's likely signings. Asked who these people were, he replied simply, "Us. And our friends." This would be Grand Royal's guiding A&R principle, at once its greatest strength and most fundamental weakness. The label allowed the band to exercise patronage, bestowing recording deals and reflected kudos on those artists it signed, and built up an aura around the band, and Mike in particular, as self-appointed, and often wilful, arbiters of cool. The label would benefit from the same skewed sense of popular cultural envelope-pushing that informed the Beasties' own records: their signing of German punk/techno trio Atari Teenage Riot was probably the label's most intuitively brilliant decision, one that remains as yet vindicated only by the fact that the group have been poached by a major label. (Atari Teenage Riot are either one of the possible futures for rock music, or an unlistenable irrelevance, just the sort of dichotomy Grand Royal seems to love. For the record, the smart money's on the former.) Sometimes, though, it seemed that the irony the Beasties exhibited in interviews, the so-uncool-it's-cool ethos they exuded since day one, was overruling notions of musical quality in the artists they decided to sign. In one *NME* article, John Mulvey described the label's back catalogue as "a stream of almost unmitigated cobblers", and while this is a harsh judgement, sales and reviews of many of the label's releases would appear to support the contention. Yet whatever criticisms can be levelled at Grand Royal's output, what the label as a whole contrived to do was help create and reinforce the idea of the Beastie Boys as being music's first family: a sort of twenty-something 1990s version of the Borgias, only without the interminable internecine bickering and power struggles. And with smaller hats.

Grand Royal also became a magazine. The initial idea had been to produce a newsletter to send to fans on the band's mailing list, but when the numbers were counted following the success of *Check Your Head*, it became clear that a charge would have to be made. "It's too expensive even doing local mailing," Mike told *Swill* as the magazine was about to launch, "so we're gonna switch over and do a subscription, quarterly kind of a thing. It just covers whatever. It has some of what we're doing and what we're up to, but it's more of a fanzine by us and about us. Every advertisement is going to be fucked up, and every article will be dissing ourselves."

Once the decision had been taken to produce an irregular but significant magazine rather than a few sheets of photocopies, it made sound commercial sense, apart from anything else, to distribute it as widely as possible. Extending the family vibe that already surrounded the band, the Beasties roped in journalist Bob Mack to edit the magazine. Mack had become part of Beastie lore after a satirical piece he'd written in *Spin* - a hip-hop map of the USA - had attracted the group's attention because he'd called them "retired rappers". Mack received a phone call from Ricky Powell to remonstrate with him, and the quick-witted scribe, blaming the comment's slant on his editor, managed to secure access to the group for a piece that would run on *Spin*'s cover coinciding with the release of *Check Your Head*. His evidently low opinion of the band's basketball ability earned him a rebuke in *Check Your Head*'s 'Skills To Pay The Bills': "Workin' on my game 'cos it's time to tax/I'm on a crazy mission to wax Bob Mack." Although the band initially kept him a little distance from their inner circle, he was an obvious choice to edit *Grand Royal* anyway. An inveterate idiosyncrasist, Mack was right at home in the off-kilter Beastie world where Billy Joel was hailed as an equal to sonic visionary Lee 'Scratch' Perry and features on demolition derbies were as likely to figure as a twenty page history of Adidas.

That Mike D should become the orchestrator of the Beasties' commercial expansion had not been immediately apparent from their past history, but he has proved to be the Beastie most adept at what the band have called "walking the dogs" - making sure things are running smoothly, taking care of business. On 'Sure Shot', the opening track of the band's fourth album, *Ill Communication*, his jibe at the media's obsession with 'slacker' culture and Generation X stereotypes as their only images of young people could equally have been his philosophy as he set up the different facets of the Grand Royal mini-empire: "Well, you say I'm twenty something and should be slacking/but I'm working harder than ever, and you could call it macking." It is worth noting that while it's true to say that Mike is the Beastie most closely tied to the running of the label, the others are involved too. "Very involved," was Adrock's description of his role in the label when speaking to *Guitar World*. "There's only three acts on the label, and I'm in two of them! Mike's president, I work A&R and MCA is treasurer." "Actually, I'm in charge of collateral," pleaded Yauch. "It's similar to treasurer, but more meaningless."

Nevertheless, Mike is the key. Doing business with him involves grappling with a complex conundrum: a rapper with a rapier wit and business sense to match who disguises his intelligence and sensibilities in his public pronouncements in favour of disseminating streams of pseudo-surreal bullshit. To describe him as unconventional is inadequate. Spike Jonze, the video director, described in a piece he wrote on the band in *Dirt* magazine how Diamond gave his cellular phone to a vagrant on a New York street rather than answer a call when he couldn't be bothered. "If it's really important they can write a letter," the Beastie maintained. Yet Mike's business strategies are smart and assured. Founded on what is basically simple common sense, he gives things that distinctive Beastie twist. In an entertaining and enlightening piece he wrote in *Dirt*, Mike summed up his business philosophy in two phrases he called "cash-isms".

"1) 'As long as they keep on makin' it, I'm gonna keep on gettin' it.' A friend of mine named Spuddie, who sold watches on an NYC street corner outside of Bloomingdale's, said that one. This is the aggressive money-harvesting attitude that keeps hard-sell kinda guys like Spuddie afloat."

"2) 'The only thing between you and other people's money is the other people.' I made that one up. It basically means there are ways to get cash if you can provide what the other people need. In essence, there's a certain amount of money in the world, and part of it is yours. How much you feel comfortable claiming and how to gain access to this currency is your problem. Money is a frame of mind, and work is selling your time to somebody else. How much your time is worth depends on what you know, and anything beyond knowing the bare essentials to garner minimum is a case scenario known as the skills to pay the bills."

There's still a part of Mike that embraces the old communist ethos: "Another approach to finance is completely avoiding it, as in learning to live on no money," he continued. "As far as I'm concerned, this is the ultimate situation: to survive without currency and be happy. I spent a few years in the no-money cycle, and it has its virtues - it frees you from the agonising humiliations that jobs can inspire. However, society at large views those without dough as relatively worthless, and you're kind of limited in terms of what you can do when it comes to entertainment, sleeping arrangements, eating and transportation. If you don't have the patience or disposition for indentured servitude or the no-money lifestyle, I advise you to go the entrepreneurial route." Adding to his portfolio, the Arthur Daley of hip-hop helped found the T-shirt company X-Large ("X-Large is a totally self-sufficient business that my partners and I built from nothing," he told *Details* in 1994, "but the appealing thing about fashion these days is that it's made by self-starter kids who seven years ago would have started a hip-hop label"). Some Beastie designs would find their way onto X-Large's books and into its hip LA store. Mike D didn't miss a trick.

Key among the virtues required to make these philosophies work is another discipline, or talent, required by rappers: the ability to improvise. "The way I look at it is, unfortunately the only way to really learn to be a good record company is by being a record company," he explained to *Swill*'s Bruce Wheeler. "And the only way for us is kinda like 'Look, we love this music, let's put it out, and we'll figure it out as it goes along and we'll learn whatever we can learn.' And that's exactly what we're doing. So we've learned a lot, and there's still a lot we have to learn."

Getting skanked by the music industry is a lesson most artists have to learn the hard way, and as a label the Beasties had to deal with it too. Adam Yauch had used a sequence of chance encounters and hastily arranged trans-American plane flights to set up the reformation of Bad Brains, the hardcore band who'd been so central to the Beasties getting together, and had inspired MCA in particular ("Darryl Jenifer is the musician who most influenced my playing," said Yauch of Bad Brains' bassist, in *Guitar World*. "Though the stuff I play now is in a different vein, if you listen to our hardcore tracks, I think you can hear his influence. I've seen them like 50 times. I climb up on something where I can get a good view of Jenifer's hands, and just jones. He's an unbelievable bassist"). Against considerable odds Yauch succeeded in getting the group back together and on course to make an album for the first time in years, only for Madonna's Maverick imprint to snatch the project away from Grand Royal after the hard work had been done.

Yauch's reaction to the situation isn't recorded, but it's likely to have been a good deal more sanguine that if the same events had transpired earlier in the band's career. After finishing a relatively uneventful world tour, and while Grand Royal was getting off the ground and Mike was building the business structures, Adam Yauch went on a journey of self-discovery not a million miles removed from some sort of tribalistic rite of passage. If he'd been an Aborigine, people would have said Yauch 'went walkabout'. Since he was a New Yorker who had relocated to California, though, people just thought he'd gone snowboarding: a pastime he'd become ardently enamoured with. There was, however, an awful lot more to it than that.

"I was just trying to learn what exists in all different cultures that is a significant part of humanity - the similarities and differences," Yauch told Gil Kaufman of the on-line rock & roll magazine *Addicted To Noise*. His quest took him to some of the world's more remote outposts. "I first went to Nepal in 1990, then I took a second trip in December of 1992 and met some Tibetan people and started to learn about the oppression and what was going on. I stopped learning about the other religions and studied Buddhism for the next four to five years."

It transpired that Adam's spiritual quest had been going on for some time. "On *Paul's Boutique* there's a song where I am starting to say what I'm feeling spiritually," he told Buddhist magazine *Shambhala Sun*. "It's called 'A Year And A Day', but the lyrics to that song aren't on the lyric sheet and I'm using a real distorted mic, so it's not really clear. And I got a lot of positive feedback from people. I was kind of taking a big risk for myself doing that, just in terms of my own confidence, but I got a lot of positivity on that. Then there were a lot of positive lyrics on *Check Your Head*. That kind of thing goes back and forth: when I hear that people are into it, it makes me feel more confident."

Yauch benefitted from the group's relocation to Los Angeles in different ways to his band mates. While Mike and Adam Horovitz bought houses, Yauch put his belongings in storage: between tours he wanted to go off snowboarding and travelling, which meant that he had little use for a home. "I'm a little bit more of a transient than the average American," he said. "I have most of my stuff in storage right now. Then I'll move to Utah to snowboard in the winter, and then I'll put it all back in storage and go on tour in the summer. [Los Angeles] doesn't feel completely like home to me. I always feel a bit like I'm visiting, like I'm waiting to get some place else." He began to realise how little he required his material possessions. Everything seemed to be pointing him in the direction of Buddhism.

Yet it wasn't simply the religious dimension that would make a profound difference to Adam's life. His experience first-hand of the strength - and serenity - in the face of brutal oppression displayed by the Tibetan people in their pacific struggle with occupying Chinese forces made him vow to use his fame and wealth to generate support for their cause. Adam met a group of Tibetan refugees while trekking in Nepal and had his eyes opened to their situation. China has occupied Tibet since 1955, citing "heaven's mandate" as their authority to do so. Tibetan people, not unreasonably, disagree, and have been systematically brutalised with a ferocity that's practically genocidal. That this situation isn't readily known about in the west probably has more to do with the numbers involved than the people. China is home to around twenty per cent of the world's population, and after years of being the most closed of communist countries, is slowly starting to open up to western capitalism. That's an awful lot of people who will potentially want to buy western-made products and services. Media corporations are well aware of this, and the Chinese government's tendency to turn prickly whenever someone criticises their human rights record is well documented. That's almost certainly the reason why Rupert Murdoch, the Australian multi-media tycoon, stopped one of his companies from publishing the memoirs of former Hong Kong governor Chris Patten, which were highly critical of the Chinese government. Murdoch understands the importance of China to the ever-increasing profitability of his business, particularly cable TV, and won't be keen to find himself blacklisted by the Chinese. For a multinational operation like his News International group of companies the implications are clear: for governments concerned with trade deficits and agricultural surpluses the mechanics of the situation are identical. So when Adam Yauch decided to try to do something to help the Tibetan people, he effectively decided to take on the world.

What the Beastie Boy set about doing is not entirely unlike what the then relatively obscure Boomtown Rats vocalist Bob Geldof achieved when, moved by images of Ethiopian famine, he decided to launch the Band Aid and Live Aid projects. Although Yauch's achievements have not had anything like the same global resonance, his work deserves to be seen in a similar light. It also raises the same question from the cynics, who will wonder why it took trips to foreign countries to open the eyes of a well-off young man that it was within his capacity to make positive changes to the world about him. Yes, Yauch could have decided to work with deprived and underprivileged people in America's inner cities or campaigned for other issues of social justice closer to home. But at least he did something - and something far more massive than pretty much anyone of his peer group. It's possible that the very geographical remoteness of Tibet helped Yauch make up his mind to get involved: issues based distant to you sometimes seem clearer cut, and, unlike many campaigns vying for public attention, there seems nothing to disagree with in the Tibetan's struggle. Also, if you wanted to be *really* uncharitable towards the Beastie Boy, you could contend that he had a greater chance to make a (reformed) name for himself by becoming involved in a relatively low-profile campaign and making it his own. But however much carping and sniping you want to indulge in, it's impossible to take away Yauch's achievements. He created the Milarepa Fund, an organisation to aid fundraising and promote awareness of the Tibetan people's struggle, and initiate and organise what has become an annual Tibetan Freedom Concert in the US. The concerts have succeeded in attracting the biggest stars in what is still mistakenly named 'alternative' music, and a measure of their success can be seen in the fact that the Chinese government moved to ban any artist involved in the concerts from releasing records in or touring China. As backhanded compliments go, this is surely the ultimate.

Yauch's decision to follow the path of Buddhism undoubtedly played a huge role in making him aware of the Tibetan people's situation, and is also likely to have massively influenced him in getting involved. With his decision to accept many Buddhist teachings (it remains unclear from his often contradictory statements in interviews whether Yauch has actually 'converted' to the religion or simply is a devoted student of it), the rapper became convinced that peaceful protest could be more effective than violence. The Tibetan struggle has been characterised by its pacifism, even in the face of quite sickening atrocities perpetrated by the occupying Chinese army. "If you can imagine the stuff that these people have undergone, that your father has been imprisoned and tortured right now, or your mother has been sterilised, or you've been gang-raped, or whatever. If you can imagine the level of torture these people have undergone, and trying to maintain a level of total compassion toward the people that are doing this to them, and not have any anger or hatred toward them, it's pretty hard," he told *Addicted To Noise*'s Kathy Mancall with uncharacteristic understatement. "This is one culture that's probably one of the most intelligent and advanced, mentally, in the world," he continued to British rock magazine *Metal Hammer*. "So advanced that they won't act or take part in any violence, they won't defend themselves physically. And to allow them to be destroyed over money makes me embarrassed to be an American. It's just disgusting."

Taking the bull by the horns, Yauch would soon make a huge contribution to the Tibetans' struggle. The establishment of the Fund and the first Tibetan Freedom Concert, though, were still a little way off. First, the Beastie Boys had another record to make.

CHAPTER NINE

"You see, Yauch wants the album done by November for April '94 release because he's on a crazy mission to snowboard all winter. Mike has taken to calling him 'The Taskmaster,' but it is not true, as Entertainment Tonight has reported, that Yauch wants to institute a series of fines within the band, à la James Brown, for unshined shoes and showing up to the studio blunted."
Bob Mack, writing in the first issue of *Grand Royal*

There was certainly something of a rush on when it came time to make the fourth Beastie album, *Ill Communication*. With *Check Your Head*'s success, the band had become hot property once again. People had even started to dress like them for the first time since the VW nonsense. "That side of it is pretty scary, that's why I'm constantly on the move," Mike told Aidin Vaziri. "One day I got the visor, next day I got the blond hair, next day I got the green hair. Always changing. Got to keep people on their toes. I figure, eventually, we'll get to the stage where the audience will get into defining their own individuality along with us, as opposed to by us. We've always been trying to get it like that, I don't know what's going on. There's plenty of room to do your own thing."

In all the excitement - hip again, with their own label, Horovitz's continuing courting of the film industry, and Yauch's immersion into Buddhism and the politics of protest - it would have been easy to ignore the central part of what had got them here. This perhaps explains the most surprising aspect of *Ill Communication*: it offered pretty few surprises. "The band's longtime friend Tim Carr (the A&R guy who signed them to Capitol) notes that in the past, the band has always taken so long to record their albums because 'they always have to reinvent the wheel,'" writes Mack at the conclusion of his piece, "'but this time,' Yauch counters philosophically, 'we're just gonna rotate the tries.'"

The band moved their equipment back to New York in May 1993 and began laying down some of the tracks that would form the basis of the new album. Thus, *Ill Communication* became an album that relied on a discourse between the group's two environments: the teeming, compact city they grew up in and the sprawling metropolis they now called home. "I think that New York is harder and more immediate, so you're constantly in contact with other people, like when you're walking around or on the trains," Yauch explained to writer Billy Miller. "You're face-to-face with people all the time. It makes the music feel a lot harder and a lot of times the music we make in LA feels more introspective - more about being in our own little world. The people I come in contact with are just our friends, and the band. Whereas in New York, you're just walking down the street by millions of people, all day. On your way to the studio you're riding the train with people everywhere. So it has a different kind of feel, more of an outward feel. The good thing about this album is we recorded part of it in New York and part of it in L.A., so it's got both of those things going on."

Another important factor in the making of *Ill Communication* was the band's long-standing desire to out-do one another when it came to knowledge of obscure and arcane musical relics, and their fascination with odd juxtapositions. While most people who are music fans will, from time to time, make tapes of their current favourite records to play themselves on a Walkman or to give to friends, the Beastie Boys had, naturally, taken this obsession to the *n*th degree. "We actually have battles to see who can make the best 'pause' tape," Yauch revealed to Miller. Naturally, they all seemed to think they did it better than their band mates. "Adrock has a pretty sweet finger on the pause button, but I'm not going to just sit back and let him walk all over me," said Yauch, throwing down a cassette-shaped gauntlet. "I've got some top-secret shit that'll blow everybody away. I'm working on this helmet that's got a tape-deck, head-phones and microphone built into it. And it's hooked up directly to my brain, so I can just think of pauses and automatically bust out. When those guys see me coming with that shit - forget about it!" Mike also bowed to Adrock's supremacy, but claimed he had the dopest music. "I might catch some flak here from the rest of the group," he admitted to *DJ Times*, "but I've got the most, the most primo records going on in the group. But Adam Horovitz will out-freak me sometimes, when it comes to looping them and sampling them and so forth." Adrock kept his counsel, but on the new album's 'Flute Loop' he made his feelings clear: "I feel like a winner when I make a mix tape/'Cause I get ill when I'm on the pause button."

Like Yauch had hinted before the record's completion, there were no massive changes to the band's style or sound on the new record. For the first time in their career, the Beastie Boys made an album that seemed like a logical follow-up to its predecessor. There were changes, but they were more subtle. Often they were to do with the type of sound the band was making, its quality and fidelity, rather than a massive alteration of musical approach. This unprecedented linear progression is a function of the shorter time it took to make the record and the fact that, for the first time, the band were working in fundamentally the same way as they had done before. It's also worth noting that the record stays similarly at arm's length from hip-hop's mainstream. With their multi-rapper tag team vocals, ill-fitting loops and SP-12 samples recalling the mid-80s hip-hop explosion, the Wu-Tang Clan had emerged to show that the the hip-hop underground could still be vibrant and vital, but they remained an exception. Gangsta rap had morphed, under the guiding hand of Dr. Dre and Snoop Doggy Dogg, into the nihilist, syrupy sounds of G-Funk, a name laying bare the music's debt to George Clinton's P-Funk (Parliament/Funkadelic) big band funk template. The sound - all analogue synth figures riding

Bernie Worrell-style keyboard bass lines - dominated hip-hop and its sonic accessibility, allied to a greater awareness within record companies of gangsta rap's marketability to white suburban teenagers, helped propel rap music to unparalleled pre-eminence. By its release in 1993, Snoop's *Doggystyle* album was easily the most anticipated record in hip-hop history. It would also become the fastest-selling, *Licensed To Ill* being rendered a distant memory. So although there was commendable and forward-looking hip-hop being made, the Beastie Boys were still somewhat non-plussed by the music they'd helped popularise. Odd records stuck out from the morass of mediocrity (Mike D went on record to profess his admiration for Nas' 1994 debut, *Illmatic*, for example), but there was no particular reason for the group to jump back in. Besides, they still had plenty of things to try out with the sound and methods of working they'd stumbled across with *Check Your Head*.

"In a lot of ways we did a lot of stuff with *Ill Communication* we wouldn't have been capable of doing before," Mike D told Aidin Vaziri. "At the same time, with *Check Your Head*, there was a lot that we learned about making a record that we applied to *Ill Communication*. This album was a lot about applying everything that we had learned on those records to this record."

"We took some time off last winter, and it started coming together real fast when we got together," Yauch explained to Billy Miller. "Not like we wrote ahead of time, but a bunch of ideas came out real fast when we hadn't really played with each other in five or six months. I guess [that happened because of] what we figured out doing our last one - the time we spent playing our instruments and trying new stuff."

"Everything's got to sound dope, so we just stay on top of it until it sounds right," he told *Guitar World*. "It's one of the most important things. We'll sit and mess around with the drums for a long time, moving the mics around, trying different EQ [graphic equaliser] settings..."

"This all comes out of the hip-hop end of what we do," Adrock interrupts. "Rock has set sounds, but hip-hop gets a little wilder. We like a lot of low-tech sounds. Everything is so high-tech these days; the sounds are so clean that they're uninteresting."

The main sound the band experimented with on *Ill Communication* was the vocals (although Yauch did begin to use an upright bass on the record, and, in that tried-and-trusted Beastie manner, his relative lack of competence made for some interesting sonic twists: "Playing the bass is my favourite shit," he rhymes on 'B-Boys Makin' It With The Freak Freak', "I might be a hack on the stand-up, but I'm working at it"). Several of the tracks find the band rapping through a Sony Karaoke Variety microphone, a snip at $35 apiece. For this refinement, the group had to thank Mario Caldato, who'd come across the device on a visit to Tokyo. "I got one and brought it back to the studio and tested it," he said in *Mix* magazine. "Everybody liked it, so I bought them all one for Christmas." As well as using broken equipment, the group recorded with it in a way most musicians would only use live. But then, if you're using a Karaoke Variety mic, there seems little point in putting it on a stand in a vocal booth and protecting it from spittle with a stretched piece of underwear fabric. So they didn't, as Yauch also relates in 'Sure Shot': "Strictly hand-held is the style I go/Never rock the mic with the panty hose".

Recorded initially in New York and mixed as they went along, *Ill Communication* is a jumbled record reflecting the craziness of its environment. In his *Dirt* feature, Spike Jonze describes the east coast studio facility the band were working in: "On one floor there is a modelling agency and on the next, a martial arts studio. We pass by the door just in time to catch a young man spinning through the air and shattering a cinder block with a flying kick. After he lands, I see he is the instructor as he bows to his kneeling pupils. When he looks up, who should it be but Yauch. Mike leads me up the

153

stairs...we enter the studio's lounge. Mario C. is standing wearing a slinky dress on top of a table in the middle of the room. He is surrounded by long, thin, beautiful creatures, models of the *Vogue* variety, who peck and paw at him, pinning and pulling his dress in a rush to perfect his outfit. Mario doesn't seem to notice as he is too wrapped up in playing Sega *PGA Tour Golf 2* with Money Mark. Except for his five o'clock shadow, he looks dashing: high heels, pearls and plunging neckline. Mark notices my confusion. 'They're having a fashion runway show downstairs. Billy Idol was supposed to model that outfit but he just sprained his ankle walking down the stairs in those heels so they grabbed Mario. He modelled in a catalogue for them last week.'"

The band had initially left LA in order to remove themselves from the distractions around G-Son and re-focus on the music: it's little wonder *Ill Communication* turned out to be such a scuffed-sounding album given the oddity of the place it was made in. Including a similar mix, as before, of explosive hardcore, dirty funk and idiosyncratic hip-hop, the record features guests of the calibre of A Tribe Called Quest's Q-Tip and the chap who Bob Mack described as "the self-proclaimed 'renaissance asshole'" Eugene Gore. A classically trained violinist, Gore lends his fiddle to the bizarre atmospheric instrumental 'Eugene's Lament', probably the only real departure from previous Beasties records. Arising, like most of the album, from a jam session in New York, the track involves Keyboard Money Mark, percussionist Eric Bobo, the Beasties and Gore. "'Eugene's Lament' was just a one-minute jam on the DAT, then we repeated a couple of sections of it and had Eugene Gore overdub violins," Mario Caldato Jr explained. "The rest of the music was straight to DAT. That's why it sounds kind of screwed up, but it came out nice." In a particularly excellent feature in *Pulse!* magazine, Michael Jarret described the track as "a meeting between classical composer George Crumb [Black Angels] and dub-master Augustus Pablo. It's enough to make one wonder," the writer concludes. What he gets by way of a response is a pretty typical display of the Beasties' pass-the-mic approach to being interviewed.

Mike D: "I hope people will wonder about it."
MCA: "We wonder about it."
Adrock: "Where'd the damn thing come from?"
Mike D: "The basic track just came."
MCA: "I wish you could see Eugene. If more people could see what Eugene looks like, they'd realise how that song is solely bridging the generation gap of the world."
Mike D: "Yeah, it is. See, you've got Bobo, who's the son of Willie Bobo - you got that lineage there - who's playing the djymbe, the most ancient instrument in the world. Mark's playing a little clave. We're all playing a little. Eugene, he's like eight years younger than us, but he's a classically trained, virtuoso-violinist kind of kid."
Adrock: "He plays Bad Brains songs on the violin."
Mike D: "He's a punk-rock violinist."
MCA: "Like at first glance, just looking at him on the street, you would think that he was definitely like a grunge kid from Seattle. He's got dreadlocks, a beard…"
Adrock: "Pearl Jam style. Crusty."
MCA: "When he grabs hold of the violin, if you didn't know, he'd start ripping some Stravinsky." Adrock: "He's Hungarian."
Mike D: "That's when he's unplugged. Plug him in, and he goes through like echoplex and all kinds of stuff. Look out! That's when he gets into the dub-violin mode. We got stuff for B-sides with Eugene that is straight-up *out*."

In that light-hearted exchange there's more about what the band think they're doing than at first appears. Mixing ancient and modern instruments, subverting the norms of the writing and recording processes, amalgamating disparate strands of musicianship, uniting generations and traditions into a distinctive, new whole - it's the band and their musical career in microcosm (minus the beer and the swearing, of course).

Another track from the opposite end of the sonic spectrum that also serves to shoe-horn several sectors of the Beastie Boys' music into one place at the same time is 'Sabotage'. A thrilling combination of their funk groove and hardcore punk approaches, it's a rudimentary song based around a monumental fuzz bass riff and some fairly meaningless lyrics shouted by Adrock ("I can't stand it, I know you planned it/But I'mma set it straight, this Watergate"). There's no chorus, just scratching that sounds like a juggernaut crunching gears, and no tune to speak of either. Yet not only does it capture their shambolic aesthetic perfectly, 'Sabotage' has become as near to a 'Fight For Your Right'-style anthem as the post-Def Jam Beasties have had. A highpoint of their live shows since *Ill Communication*'s release, the song now typically closes them, or at least finds its way into an encore. The accompanying video, directed by Spike Jonze, was also instrumental in securing the band much of the counterculture credibility they enjoy today. Filmed on the streets of Los Angeles, the band appear as a selection of characters straight out of a made-up *Starsky & Hutch*-type '70s TV cop show. Not particularly representative of the band or the album, 'Sabotage' nevertheless has become, for many of their present audience, the song and the image that defines the Beastie Boys. The contrariness of this arrangement seems apt.

Like *Check Your Head*, *Ill Communication* was condensed from oodles of tape, though this time the band weren't quite as prolific. Then again, they didn't spend as much time simply laying down jams, and having already made an album in this way before they were much clearer about what they wanted and how to go about getting it. They produced a mere twenty hours of digital tape. Unsurprisingly, given that they were trying to achieve a raw feel and dirty sound, many of the rough mixes done early in the recording process, at the New York studio, Tin Pan Alley, where they first started work on the album, ended up on the finished record. "We make mixes and listen to 'em, live with 'em," Caldato explained to *Mix*: "We try a lot of shit, and if it works, it works. There are a lot of ideas in the group, and I throw in some, too. A lot of times, we end up going with our gut feelings, like using rough mixes. The stuff that we spend more time on doesn't come out as hype. It's weird. If it's there, it's there - it comes out by itself."

And like the sounds and performances, this time some messages come leaping out of the record. It's this that elevates *Ill Communication* above the status of simply being *Check Your Head Part II*. Like the title suggests, the Beasties clearly decided that, beneath all the distorted mics and crackling sonics, this was the time to start speaking to their audience. They would write their lyrics separately, bringing them together during recording, which meant that each voice tends to get a few lines on its own rather than get aurally complicated by the other two. This cancels out some of the distraction the distorted vocals give the lyrics and makes the songs sound more comprehensible, allowing the band to get points made regardless of the confusing surface detail. 'Sure Shot' opens the album with an unequivocal Yauch calling time on the lunacy and sexism of his and his band's past, and sending out a clear message to other rappers that it was high time the genre started treating women with a great deal more respect (interestingly, the much-misunderstood Tupac Shakur had been thinking along similar lines; his 'Dear Mama' single of the same year was a similarly powerful plea extended into an entire song, and addressed to his ex-drug addict mother). Freed from the need to be performing a role, allowed finally by the music that was supposed to be a release in the first place to be himself in public, Yauch makes up for lost time. On 'The Update', a passionate defence of a polluted planet, he examines his inner self and lays bare the advice he can give from the journey he'd taken: "I took control of my life, just as anyone can/I want everyone to see it's in the palm of your hand."

Ill Communication isn't completely serious - it's a Beastie Boys album, how could it be? Thus the trashy thrash of 'Tough Guy', about a bloke with a bad attitude on the basketball court, is typically goofy, and the album finds Adrock, in particular, specialising in some hilarious one-liners. They continued to prefer to have a ball and act the goat rather than indulge in a straightforward exchange with the world's press. According to Johnny Dee, writing one of what was, even by the group's considerable standards, a particularly hilarious feature in *NME*, the band's visit to Japan on the world tour they undertook to promote *Ill Communication* made for some interesting culture clashes. In one restaurant, the menu had been translated into English with predictable consequences. The local cuisine included Grated Foamy Yam, A Piece Of Cooked Devil's Tongue Jelly and Noodles In A Bowl Of Ice Cold Water. The band and Dee managed the staggering feat of accidentally bumping into one another in Tokyo, a city of eleven million people, but they seemed to treat this as an entirely rational occurrence. Somewhat unsurprisingly, record shopping was high on the agenda: "Japan is brilliant for vinyl," Mike told Dee. "There's all this rare stuff that I've been looking two years for, and you walk into a store and you find it straight away. But it costs 200 bucks, so there's this thing where you think, 'Do you buy it?' 'cos if you do every time you play it you're just gonna to be thinking of the 200 bucks."He pauses and considers briefly. "You buy it every time." Arriving at a Tokyo venue, the band were showered with gifts, one female fan handing Mike an envelope. On opening it he found three photos of the girl who'd given it to him in her pyjamas, brandishing copies of the band's albums. Adrock described the pictures as "Freaky fuckin' deaky."

Ill Communication is a record more than any other of the band's career that revels in the tensions that spring from this constant battle between the Beasties' serious intentions and their helplessly playful manner. It struggles to get its point across because it can't always keep a straight face. But it does get deep, and it relies on all three rappers to bring their parts of the group personality into play. But *Ill Communication*'s illest communications are always Yauch's. In 'Alright Hear This', wherein the band pay tribute to many of the jazz and funk musicians whose beats and basslines they've sampled and whose music has continued to spur their own creativity onwards, MCA raps, "In these times of melding cultures/I give respect for what's been borrowed and lent/I know this music comes down from African descent". Even when he's being jocular he's saying something about his philosophical transformation and his changing life. 'Sure Shot' finds him coyly admitting to an outbreak of grey hair, though even this is twisted around and turned into an emcee brag.

If his lyrics weren't evidence enough of the changes Adam had made to his life, the tracks 'Bodhisattva Vow' and 'Shambala' forced him to alter it even more. These tracks use samples of Tibetan monks utilising a vocal technique called 'overtoning' in the west, which Yauch wanted to make sure they were paid for. If the band were to pay American musicians whose work they'd sampled, he reasoned, it was logical and fair that people whose traditional music he'd used should see the benefit of it as well. The problem was how to compensate someone whose identity you didn't know, and whose country was occupied. Yauch got in touch with American student Erin Potts, whom he'd met while in Nepal.

Potts told *Addicted To Noise*: "He was on holiday and I was studying there. I took him around one day to the Tibetan part of town and he got really excited about it. That was in December 1992, and we just stayed in contact. When I came back, the Beastie Boys had done two songs on [*Ill Communication*] which used samples from Tibetan monks and other things, and they wanted to put the royalties aside from those songs to give back to the Tibetan people. So they asked me if I'd help distribute the money. We talked about it, and decided the best way would be to set up a foundation that would distribute money and educate people at the same time."

Yauch and Potts set up the Milarepa Fund in May 1994 with the intention of, among other things, using money raised to sponsor Tibetan children through US schools. It also donates money to other Tibetan charitable organisations whose work has been ongoing and whose infrastructures mean it will best help those it's intended to reach. But just as important is the fact that Milarepa educates the public at large about the Tibetan people's plight. "The more money that a Tibetan organisation receives, the more they can raise awareness about the Tibetan culture and political situation," Potts continues. "We're pretty excited about giving money to educational things. That's where most of our money has gone in the past. We've done things like an educational package for teachers and students for the classroom, everywhere from the kindergarten to college level. The more we can directly help the Tibetan people, and the more we can educate non-Tibetan people about what's going on in Tibet, the quicker we'll get to a point where we won't have to give the Tibetan people money anymore, because they'll be self-sufficient."

The Fund remains realistic about how its work can influence the situation. Potts and Yauch didn't expect Beastie Boys fans to start organising pickets of local congressmen or start giving all their spare time to the cause just because they'd heard about it on a record. But there are still things they think people can assist with on a personal, individual level. "The first thing, and in some ways the easiest and in some ways the hardest, is just not to buy any products made in China," explained Potts to *ATN*'s Kathy Mancall. "Products that are produced in China have a chance of being produced in slave labour camps, where political prisoners are forced to make, like, tube socks and toys and things like that. There are about eight to ten million prisoners who are forced to labour for some of the products which come to the United States. That money is going to oppression."

Yauch had proved that one person can make a difference, catalysing those around him to the good of a cause he believed in passionately. The next challenge was how to involve the Beastie Boys' audience. Although benefit gigs would have been logical, Yauch was thinking bigger. Enlisting major names such as the Smashing Pumpkins, Rage Against The Machine, Bjork and Sonic Youth, the Beasties initiated the Tibetan Freedom Concert, held over two summer days at Golden Gate Park in San Francisco in 1996. 100,000 people paid almost $30 per day, money which flowed back into Milarepa's coffers. The cause definitely united the artists, which begs the question as to why no one had tried to do it before. The fact remains that no one else had considered it until Adam Yauch, let alone managed to pull it all together. Into the bargain, he managed to get a bunch of rock stars not always known for their forthcoming natures to talk to the world's press about the Tibetan situation. Billy Corgan of the Smashing Pumpkins spoke for many when he was interviewed by *Addicted To Noise*: "All praise to Adam from the Beastie Boys for helping people focus on this and giving people like us something to connect to it, 'cause you don't really know where to start or end with something like this."

The Tibetan Freedom Concert made waves and raised cash, but it did much more besides. It proved that the "slacker generation" cared more about what was going on across the face of the planet than the people supposedly in charge of it. And while, as Sonic Youth's Lee Renaldo postulated to Mancall, this was the first time enough like-minded, vaguely underground bands had been successful enough to corral them all together in a field for a weekend and get enough people come along in support of a single cause to make it worthwhile, it's still little short of staggering that the man who made it all happen was MCA out of the Beastie Boys. Now *that's* ill.

Although the Freedom Concert earned the Tibetan cause more coverage across a much wider range of media than it had ever had before, it failed to produce a groundswell of public opinion large enough to deflect the American government from its course. Depressingly, if unsurprisingly, China was granted Most Favoured Nation trading status days after the concert. Yauch was furious. "It's an outrage," he told Kathy Mancall, in *Addicted To Noise*'s excellent and definitive feature on the trials and tribulations everyone concerned suffered to make the concert happen. "It once again exemplifies that our elected officials are working in the interest of big business and not working in the interest of humanity, not working in the interest of the American people. Those people who choose to make an argument solely on a business level and ignore human rights - you know, that it's creating jobs or helping the American economy - they're wrong. It's actually creating more of a deficit in the American economy. It's taking away American jobs. Like Boeing started doing business in China, then started a factory there and shut down an entire factory in America, where thousands of people were getting paid $30 an hour, or whatever they got paid, and now they're [Boeing] only paying a couple of dollars an hour. So now the trade that's going on is actually damaging the American economy directly. The only people that are profiting from this are a select few upper-echelon people who run our corporations. Our government is run by big business, not by the people. [Tibetan] culture's going to be wiped out. There's only a couple of years left. At the rate that their genocide is going, at the rate that they're operating the influx of Chinese, population transfer policies, and the rate that they're going around sterilising women in trucks, doing forced abortions, tearing down buildings, there's only a couple of years left for Tibet. My hopes are, that in a year from now, when Most Favoured Nation status comes up, that everyone will be up in arms about this, that there will be demonstrations in campuses around the world, and that the people of America will no longer allow corporations to guide our government."

Despite the very serious issues the group raised with *Ill Communication* and their various activities surrounding it, the record may well end up being looked upon as a much-needed injection of light, humour and hope into a year that threatened to bring alternative music's house of cards crashing down. The suicide of Nirvana singer Kurt Cobain provided a generation with a James Dean-like icon to gaze down balefully from student bedroom walls worldwide: in the same way that Tupac Shakur's murder two years later would affect hip-hop, Cobain's death initially stunned the alternative music world, and although a different type of attitude would eventually seem to assert itself in the guitar-based left-field music made after 1994, *Ill Communication* arrived at a time when all there seemed to be in Nirvana's absence was a vacuum. That they made a record that seemed to suggest limitless possibilities both for them and for us, a record that reminds you to delight in your life however crazy or messed up it might seem, could well be one of the most significant achievements of their long and multi-faceted career. In his excellent Japan piece in *NME*, Johnny Dee wrote: "In 1994, the year that will be remembered for Kurt Cobain's suicide, the Beastie Boys kept our faith alive, our belief, basically, that pop music is a daft, stupid thing to do and own. They reminded us that music can be fun, that you can make the mad, all-over-the-place record you want to make and still be celebrated. The Beastie Boys make everyone under the age of 30 want to start a band and be much like them - three mates mooching around the world." That this is just a small part of the Beasties' legacy is all the more remarkable.

After *Ill Communication*'s release and a splenetically well-received world tour, the Beasties concocted a sleeve that parodied a number of stylish and collectable Moog keyboard albums from France in the 1970s and wrapped it around a CD of instrumentals from their last two LPs. Initially conceived as a promotional item, it became collectable and started changing hands for exorbitant sums, so Grand Royal released it in 1996. The band called it *The In Sound From Way Out!*, and whether it was or not depended really on how much you'd bought into the notion that the group were infallible genii (it wasn't; they weren't). One review, in *NME*, said that "releasing an album of instrumental versions of B-sides, filler sections and out-takes of the last two albums is like giving someone half a bag of Sainsbury's self-raising flour and telling them it's a cake". The sleevenotes, written in a sort of lazily messed-up approximation of French, were hilarious. Oddly, the record helped cement a relationship that had been brewing between Grand Royal and ultra-credible British instrumental hip-hop label Mo' Wax. The latter would release two albums by the Beasties' keyboard whizz, Money Mark, and the label's founder, James Lavelle, was one of a group of London DJs who helped bring back into clubland fashion the various experimental Moog records the Beasties were referencing. *Grand Royal* magazine duly did a cover story on Moogs. And guess what? Experimental French dance music, most of it made on outmoded keyboards, became one of Europe's biggest sounds over the next couple of years, as groups like Daft Punk and Air enjoyed chart hits that must have been beyond their wildest imaginings. The self-perpetuating cool/uncool enigma the band had created now had its own incalculable momentum. The Beastie Boys have a lot to answer for.

CHAPTER TEN

"You'll be like, 'Hello, nasty - where you been?
It's time you brought the grimy beats out The Dungeon'."

Lisbon, Portugal, May 1998. Adrock, Mike D and MCA sit across a table from half a dozen European journalists. The throng are gathered because the Beastie Boys have just completed their long-awaited and feverishly anticipated new LP. Called *Hello Nasty*, and played for the first time to the journalists the day before, it is a mammoth twenty-plus track mélange of keyboard-driven balladeering and scatological hip-hop. Impossible to assimilate in a single sitting, especially when that sitting is in a room with a bunch of other people who are talking, the journalists at the press conference are understandably unsure of what to ask the group about the record. That it is both the primary reason for everyone to be here and simultaneously the thing that no-one is able to talk about seems to be a quite typically Beastie conundrum. Questions, therefore, range from the sublime to the ridiculous as the European press corps attempt to get some information out of the band. They have their moments of success, but overall the situation is tailor-made for the Beastie Boys to indulge in their favourite pastime - talking complete and utter shite.

Adrock: "In 1704, what happened was they were bringing oxen over for the President of Portugal to Lisbon and the ship sank, and they took the…bison, did I say? Or aardvark? - and stuffed it and gave it to the Pope."
MCA: "We had a guy telling us the history of Lisbon, though we thought he probably made it all up."
Adrock: "He said that Portugal is the second largest

rice-consuming nation in the world…"

Mike D: "…behind China…"

Adrock: "…and I don't believe that."

Mike D: "I second guessed him on the spot, and I countered that Japan or some of the other Asian countries would be ahead of Portugal."

MCA: "To which he responded, 'No, they eat raw fish.' That was his theory."

Mike D: "Which is true. However, I don't think he was accounting for combining the raw fish with rice - hence, sushi. Hence is from a Portuguese word."

Adrock: "It's the second most used word in Lisbon. It was brought over on a boat."

Mike D: "It was sailor speak. Vasco da Gama used to say 'Hance! Hance!' to his crew, which made them drop their drawers, and in turn it got reinterpreted, and it got co-opted into English because the Portuguese Queen married an Englishman, and she told him to 'hance', and he misinterpreted it and it became 'hence'. I actually had to undergo extensive plastic surgery since finishing the album two weeks ago, and I've recovered miraculously well. This was one of the reasons we came here to Lisbon, because Lisbon is actually the third most popular city for plastic surgery in the world. And they started early too - it was actually the eleventh King in 1848, he had an accident and needed to have his face reconstructed, and he was one of the first European monarchs to have plastic surgery."

MCA: "Fascinating… he blows me away."

Journalist: "What about the rumour you started that you have made three different albums, and that one of them was recorded in a submarine?"

Adrock: "They put that in the paper? That's top secret information."

Mike D: "It was a secret mission."

MCA: "We're gonna have to ask that this information remains

secret. If everyone's sworn to secrecy, there was one album that was recorded in a submarine. But that album, we just actually made the whole record out of gold and put it in a satellite and launched it out into space, hoping that some lifeform out there'll find it and be able to get into it."

Adrock: "And the other one was stuffed for the Pope."

MCA: "And the other one drowned on its way here."

Adrock: "It slipped out of the submarine and drowned."

MCA: "That album is disguised as a stuffed rhinoceros."

Adrock: "It's actually in the museum in Lisbon, which is the fourth smallest museum in the world."

Mike D: "Going back to Vasco de Gama's time, he had seen that the world was round and he figured that architecture should reflect that. Because if we continued building these 90 degree angle buildings we would believe the earth was flat."

Adrock: "The remarkable thing about this man is that he is the second lightest man ever to live in the world, weighing four pounds."

Mike D: "Could he fit in your pocket?"

Adrock: "No! Regular stance! 6-4."

Mike D: "So he was made of, like, different matter…?"

Adrock: "Hey, I dunno, it was a long time ago!"

Journalist: "Why did it take so long for the new LP to get finished? Was it that you waited that long because you wanted to be ready for the world championships of soccer?"

MCA: "That's what it was. We actually finished about two or three years ago but we were waiting."

Mike D: "We were looking for a big event to time it with, *a la* Michael Jackson and Madonna, they always synchronise their releases with big things. And we thought, World Cup '98 - that's us! It had us written all over it, pretty much."

MCA: "A lot of people in the football community are talking about us!"

Mike D: "People don't know that when we were recording the vocals we were wearing long socks, short shorts, and those pads they wear under their socks. While we were doing the vocals. To get into the mood of the whole World Cup…"

…and so on. Remarkably, the band did manage to communicate a fair amount of information about *Hello Nasty* and how it was made, but that was more by accident than design. "I don't know why anyone would even want to talk seriously with us when we're like that," Mike admitted to *NME*'s Ted Kessler. The fact that the band had invited people to try seemed to have eluded him. Yet the fact that the three of them act like twits when they're together had a major effect on the sound of the new LP, in particular on the rhymes and the delivery of the vocals.

The band's tendency to freestyle their way through interviews is irritating for anyone who wants to try to get to the heart of what they're about, but in itself it's quite revealing. Where people like Bob Dylan have made an art form out of their elusive conversational nature, the Beasties' interview technique seems to be a direct result of their hip-hop upbringing. Just as they have to be able to improvise rhymes, emcees ought to be able to quickly come up with the sort of nonsense the Beasties regularly foist on the press. The stream-of-consciousness rambling, and the role playing they've spent over a decade honing, is so much a part of what they're about that it has become second nature. It also impacts on their creativity in a positive manner.

"We started off doing stuff we haven't done since *Paul's Boutique*," Mike explained to Kessler. "Like, we were hanging out at each other's apartments working on lyrics together for the first time in years, so our voices just drop in and out a lot and we sing each other's rhymes. The last two albums we'd turn up with our parts pretty much written, but this was more fun. I think we try and get a balance when we write. There's something that happens when we get together and start writing rhymes. We go for integrating the goofing around that comes with us three being in the same room, and the serious intent. I hope."

"We are definitely dropping some styles we've never dropped before," Mike had told *NME* of the new record when interviewed for a news piece in December 1997. "But at the same time, we're going to rhyme school and on that end we are doing some stuff that perhaps only we uniquely can do."

"On this [album] we went back to switching up a lot more of the rhymes," MCA opined at the Lisbon conference. "On the last two we didn't do as much of that." For the first time since *Paul's Boutique* the Beasties give full rein to their tag team tendencies, rhyming off one another with an almost audible glee. The voices have changed a little, too - Adrock is hoarser, Mike warmer - but it's the playful interaction between them that immediately strikes the listener. The difference to *Ill Communication* is particularly marked: there the verses would almost split into three, as each rapper delivered typically a four line stanza that would often have little thematic connection to the lyrics the other two were dropping adjacent to it. But here, writing together once again, they are able to exploit the full range of their talents as emcees.

The cleaner vocal sound also makes a difference, and reinforces notions of the record's kinship with *Paul's Boutique*. Referring back to MCA's lines on 'Sure Shot' (where he spoke about their preference at that time for distorting microphones held in the hand and recorded without protection from spittle), and emphasising the decision to use a clean vocal sound, Mike expounds on the techniques used to record the vocals on *Hello Nasty*. "We used the panty hose - and I mean that in all due respect - technique on the microphones. On our last couple of albums we used these special mics that were built for us that had a certain distorted sound, but this time we went back to a high quality Sennheiser, a German microphone, with the panty hose in front of it to avoid any pops, any unwanted things of that nature. We spent a lot of time hanging out at each other's apartments, working on rhymes together and splitting 'em up, instead of each coming in with our own thing."

Recorded at several New York locations, including Sean Lennon's loft and The Dungeon, the band's subterranean rehearsal space, the record involved the trio plus regular hands Caldato, Nishita and Bobo. Extra vocalists were also deployed, though this time there were no rappers from outside the Beastie set-up. Miho from the Grand Royal-signed Cibo Mato and Luscious Jackson's Jill Cuniff appeared alongside Brooke Williams on a selection of the more conventional songs on the album. But by far the band's biggest coup was in securing the services of the legendary dub visionary Lee 'Scratch' Perry. Speaking in Lisbon about the guests, Mike singled the Jamaican out from the line-up of friends and accomplices. "Lee Perry is the exception, 'cos he was just someone who we probably would never have dreamed of ever having the opportunity to work with, he was definitely a big inspiration and influence or whatever on us, but we thought of him up on this certain level. I never imagined, listening to his records, that we'd ever do any kind of collaboration together."

When *Grand Royal 2* arrived with Perry on the cover, the dubmeister was merely a respected and influential pioneer of instrumental reggae with little real currency beyond the genre in anything other than name. The exceptions had been provided by The Clash, who enlisted him to produce their 'Complete Control' single in 1978 at the height of punk's love affair with reggae, and over a decade later by the Prodigy, who sampled a portion of a record he'd produced in 1976 for Max Romeo, 'Chase The Devil', and used it as the hookline for their hit single 'Out Of Space'. Even then, those were still reference points that had a far greater resonance in Britain than in the US, where *Grand Royal* sold most copies. In magazine publishing, where the choice of cover can make or break a title's viability, the decision could be viewed as either courageous or foolhardy. Yet it would stand as yet another example of the Beasties' uncanny knack for pre-empting trends in contemporary culture.

Partly as a result of some well-received European festival

appearances, and partly because of the impact made by Island Records' release of the *Arkology* box set which collated key musical moments from Perry's Black Ark studios on three CDs, Perry's star was very firmly in the ascendant in 1998, particularly among the alternative crowd the Beasties had the strongest appeal to. In terms of conventional career structures and power moves, you'd normally have expected an artist of Perry's stature to jump at the chance of working on one of the most talked-about LPs of the year. But Perry is anything but conventional: this is a man who once set up a microphone to record a palm tree. Living the life of a recluse in Switzerland, rare interviews with the producer had shown him to be either calculatedly wacky or completely unhinged. His life had been peppered with bizarre occurrences. For example, at the height of his production powers in the late '70s, his Black Ark studio was razed to the ground, and there are many people in his native Jamaica who allege that Perry torched it himself. For several days earlier, he had been spotted walking backwards around the streets of Kingston beating the ground repeatedly with a hammer. He exhibited many of the same sort of creatively productive extremes that the Beasties did, but given his ways and his venerability, the group were perhaps a little wary of approaching him directly. Yet an instrumental track they'd called 'Dr. Lee' seemed to provide too good an opportunity to miss. "We've looked up to Lee for a long time, and we'd recorded a track that we thought sounded a lot like Lee Perry when we first recorded it," elaborated Adrock in Lisbon. "Then Mario had the idea of actually getting in touch with him to get him to do vocals on it, which we all thought was incredible but we had no idea it would actually happen. And then..."

"We played a show in Tokyo with him and he got on stage with us," Mike recalls. "Then we met him in Hong Kong, and he had a hat on and he took off his hat and he had a whole stack o' lyrics in his hat. He had glued crystals and CDs and mirrors all over it too. Then he played the Tibetan Freedom

Concert. But it was last Halloween [October 31st, 1997, coincidentally, Adam Horovitz's 31st birthday] when he actually came to record his vocal. Lee Perry has his whole style or his own technique of dressing, he has these boots and his hat covered with mirrors. And it was Halloween, so all the other humans around were wearing their own unique style, so it didn't look any different to anyone else. He'd written all his lyrics on the back of a poster for a show and he came down…Mario had kind of described to him what the track was like and he came down, heard it and got right into it and did it."

"He was cool," Yauch remembers. "He had a bunch o' lyrics written out and Mario had a mic set up for him. He listened to a little bit of the track, and he was just like, 'Okay! Rewind! Rewind! Punch me in!' And he just sang one whole take and then he wanted to sing another one. Then he sang another one, and most of the lyrics were completely different on the second one, I think he was mostly improvising. Then he did a whole load of ad-libs, and what's on the record is basically the whole second take with a bunch of ad-libs thrown in. He's cool. He just has a nice vibe about him, he's just a really interesting dude. He's quite a punk too. And maybe being eccentric allows him to be more creative with music: he's not self-conscious so he just goes off, makes crazy sounds. Our friend Ricky [Powell] stopped by when Lee Perry was on the mic, and I don't think Ricky really knew who he was. Lee was making all these crazy sounds and Ricky was just…"

"Ricky didn't have headphones so he couldn't hear the mix, so it just sounded like Lee Perry was making all these crazy sounds," Mike clarifies, "but when we listened back in the mix, most of the things he did really made sense, and he put them in specific places to go with the vocals, so he had a whole concept goin' on.

"The two times I met him he just did his thing," Horovitz concludes. "Just the way he looked, or his fashion sense, was punk, and the way that he carried himself."

There was one other important new face in the Beasties' '98 line-up which greatly added to their in-depth strength. As much as their rapping styles were constantly pushing back the boundaries, their scratch techniques had lagged behind. That they decided to do something about it on *Hello Nasty* is hardly surprising: they have always sought to be at the cutting edge of hip-hop production, and the emergence of some genuinely startling turntable experimentalists through the '90s meant that it was a part of their music that could no longer be ignored. Unsurprisingly, when looking at how to move this part of their sound onwards, the Beasties went straight to the top.

The band decided to use the skills of Mix Master Mike to garnish their album and subsequent touring with state-of-the-art decknology. A member of the three-man Bay Area DJ team, the Invisibl Skratch Picklz, Mike is widely regarded as one of the finest scratchmix DJs ever, and is credited with innovations to the art that include using a wah-wah pedal while scratching. In keeping with the friends-together vibe that permeated their records since the beginning of the decade, though, the Beasties didn't just look Mike up in a big hip-hop phone book. The DJ had met Adam Yauch at, suitably, the annual reunion of old school breakdance legends the Rock Steady Crew, and the twosome had kept in touch by telephone. "Mix Master Mike is no joke on the turntables," Yauch said during an internet chat on America On Line in 1997. "I'm sure we'll at least include one of his answering machine messages to me on the record, as those are equally impressive." It's one of these messages that opens 'Three MCs And One DJ'.

"I used to call him up and leave crazy scratch messages on his answerphone," the DJ confirms. "And eventually they all gave me a call and said, 'Come down and work with us, we've got scratching on the next album and we need to take our shit on to the next level on that'. And so they flew me out there [to New York] to do the album."

On arriving in NYC, Mike spent a mere five days working on his parts of the record. Things got off to a flying start.

Inspired by Mike's techniques the band improvised a track in a couple of hours that made it on to the finished LP. "I was cutting a drum, right?" the Mix Master recalls, by which he means that he was creating a drum beat using the drum sound from a record and manipulating the one record and his mixer to produce a pattern like a drum machine. "Everybody was just watching me - they used to stop the sessions and everyone used to just watch me do my shit. And them three were like, 'We'll be *right* back!' They went to the living room in RPM studios and they were writing, and they called me in there and told me the hook - 'three emcees and one deejay' - and I was like, it sounded kinda corny to me at first! Then Adrock said 'Find something that rhymes with 'hey' or 'say.'' So I put together all the drops - 'Mix Master Mike, whatcha got to say?' - all of those. And I cut the drum live. They rhymed. And it just came out! Those guys are fuckin' geniuses. That track was really special - it just came together out of the blue."

A sample Mike scratched into the track's first chorus from Snoop Doggy Dogg's 'Gin And Juice' - the words "every single day" - had to be removed from the final LP after Snoop's former label, Death Row, would only grant sample clearance in return for a prohibitively massive sum. "It worked so good with that [sample] - it broke my heart we had to change it," the DJ says. "But Adam threw in something that was really funny...so at this point, I sample strategically. I don't sample hooks - I usually just say them myself through an effects processor and then [make an acetate and] cut them up." One is reminded of another line on the album, Yauch opining that "it starts with the greed and then goes all wrong/That's why we can't all just get along". Mike thinks things should be more family-oriented, and if he scratches a piece of someone's record into the chorus of a Beastie Boys track, payment in kind - him doing cuts on a track by the person being sampled - would be much more appropriate. He clearly fits right in to the Beasties set-up.

"I've always followed them," he admits. "I was always a fan

and they were always special to me so I knew their capabilities already. I feel very much at home with them, like I shoulda been there from the get-go maybe! Not taking anything away from Hurricane, but that was their missing ingredient. Actually, he was involved in none of the records before. Most of the scratches were done by Adrock and MCA. Mostly Adrock though."

There were no hardcore tracks this time, eight of the fourteen or so the band had recorded early in the album's gestation having already been released on Grand Royal as the *Aglio E Olio* EP. Named after the most common dish in Italy (pasta with oil), the EP freed the band from what, with hindsight, appears to have been the limitation of having to include the punk material alongside the other music they were making on *Ill Communication*. It is no coincidence that *Hello Nasty* is a sharper and more focused record as a result. ("None of our records are as well-focused as people assume," Diamond told Kessler. "When we start making a record we're not that together, it's more whatever happens. We don't have a comprehensive scheme.")

So *Hello Nasty* is the first Beasties album that can be seen as anything other than a step onwards and outwards from their previous work. Dispensing with the hardcore tracks is only a part of it: in its concentration on quickly changing beats, chopped-up loops and a hyped-up, interactive rapping style, the majority of the record bears close resemblance to *Paul's Boutique* and its relentless quest to redefine its own shapes and textures. It feels like the album they had spent their whole lives working towards.

"Hip-hop has gone beyond taking a bar or half a bar and freaking it," Mike told the Portuguese conference. "This programming's kinda pretty complex but it's exciting." Yet what Mike here analyses as a very up-to-date manner of making hip-hop was, for the band, the product of an older style of working. The mix-tape battles that had informed *Check*

Your Head were replaced by a competitive quest to find the sharpest samples and condense them as densely as possible. On the rap tracks that form the majority of the record, this is the main defining feature, and the band's lyric writing homes in on the point. Even the titles belie it: 'Super Disco Breakin'', the album's first track, is in itself a reference to the sample collector's treasure trove of compilation albums featuring tracks with breakbeats in them released early in the '80s, called *Super Disco Brakes*.

Lyrical highlights are legion, though the best rhymes are often the result of the occasions the band muse on the creative process. Adrock - so long in the shadows while his band mates had spent their time building up their portfolios of extracurricular activities - emerges from the background as the beat-head extraordinaire. As his band mates knew, his time out of the spotlight hadn't all been consumed by the handful of film roles he'd accepted: he told Ted Kessler that "it would be kinda sad to say that playing with old keyboards and drum machines is what I like to do in my spare time, but sadly it's true." His lyrics about making music are some of the best on the record.

In 'Unite', Adrock compares his beatmaking skills to the robotic efficiency of an ancient drum machine: "When it comes to beats, well I'm the Rhythm Ace". During 'No Shame In My Game', he raps, "I'm the Benihana chef on the SP-12/Chop the fuck out the beats left on the shelf". That the band had gone back to using the short sample-time beat box of yore helps to explain the record's move back to briefer sampled loops; that Adrock - acknowledged within the group as the master of these things ("Adam Horovitz, well, he's consumed by music. All day long he's making beats and playing with guitars, drum machines," Mike told *NME* in December '97) - compares his beat-chopping to a particularly adept Japanese cook is a clever but highly informative metaphor. It's funny, too, and as such is a neat exemplar of what the band do throughout the album. Lyrically they offer funky little clues and direction pointers, they talk a bit about stuff that's on their minds, they hint at themes and messages while mainly avoiding anything explicit.

There are, though, pieces of self-revelation scattered about the record, particularly in the final track that finds Horovitz pining for his mother, who died after losing her battle with alcoholism when Adrock was eighteen, and asking for the 'Instant Death' of the song's title. That he feels, if not comfortable, at least able to get these things off his chest, confirms that the music he and his band are making has reached a point where he feels secure enough to unburden himself. "Yeah, it's autobiographical," he admitted to Kessler, "but it's pretty explicit, I don't need to go into details. If you're not honest in what you write, people will only make up what's not between the lines. Actually, that song and 'And Me' were easier than any of the rhymes to write, because they're only, like, three lines." The slower and more song-based material, whether sung by the band or their guest vocalists, is more reflective and a little heavier than the majority of the raps, where rhymes are encouraged to veer off on tangential trajectories like true off-the-head free-associative freestyles while the threads get tied together for strange choruses that dot the mix.

'Putting Shame In Your Game' is typically complex and dense but still remains relaxed. The central theme is based on a play on words. The title is a phrase that crops up occasionally in hip-hop records: if someone is putting shame in your game, they're showing you up as not being as good at what you're doing as you think you are. The Beasties do this but they pepper the lyric with references to various board games and toys, deliberately misinterpreting "game" literally rather than, in this context, its use as a synonym for "business". Thus boomerangs, Lotto and Lego get mentioned alongside a certain word game. Where *Paul's Boutique* had ping-pong and, they claim, *Ill Communication* was constructed between games of dominoes, the Beasties are here waxing lyrical about their prowess at Boggle. Or, at any rate, Adrock is. Referencing Run

DMC's 'King Of Rock' ("I'm the king of rock, there is none higher/Sucker emcees must call me sire"), he brags about his prowess: "I'm the king of Boggle, there is none higher/I get eleven points off the word 'quagmire'". Mike talks about listening to the track on a Walkman and getting "so hyped", while Yauch leavens the laughs with a bullish quatrain about how he won't sell music for multinationals to use in adverts. Does it make any difference? Is the serious stuff not buried under the weight of the silliness and jocularity? Yauch doesn't think so. "Every thought in the mind is a planted seed," he intones.

There are lyrics that reinforce the band's place in rap history ('Intergalactic' finds them talking about being "from the family tree of old school hip-hop", while references to breakdancing, "body rock", *Krush Groove* - a mid-80s rap film in which the band made a brief appearance - and *Wild Style* crop up all over the place, others that find them being wry about their businesses ("So I plan and I scam and write it off on my taxes") and some fine battle rhymes ("You've got gall…to step to me, I'm a rapophile/If you battle me you're in denial"). No matter how random some of the thoughts seem to be, they always have the happy knack of arriving back somewhere near the point: referring to old school master Kool Moe Dee as if he'd been grading his raps, Mike says he "got an A from Moe Dee for sticking to themes". And the band are supremely artful in the poetic construction of the lyrics. 'The Negotiation Limerick File' is, strangely enough, a sequence of limericks about negotiation. 'Intergalactic' has three verses, each using a single rhyme sound (in the first it's "dial", "style" and "exile" while the third allows them to rhyme "flop", "hip-hop" and "wok" with a portion of *Licensed To Ill* track 'The New Style', where Adrock lets the beat "mmmmm, drop"). Although Beastie friend and collaborator Q-Tip and his group A Tribe Called Quest did the same thing on their Lou Reed-sampling global hit single 'Can I Kick It?', their rhymes were join-the-dots simple by comparison.

Hello Nasty crystalises what makes the Beasties so fresh and exciting as rap style innovators: their massive talent is allied to a basically playful nature to produce music that is almost apoplectic in its urgency to communicate the joys of its creation. The album is the sound of the Beastie Boys revelling in rhymes. And it's also a record borne of times when such behaviour is able to make a bigger impact than ever before.

Released into the middle of the biggest revival in the fortunes of hip-hop's original attitudes that the music has witnessed, *Hello Nasty* was impeccably timed. The album's first single, 'Intergalactic', debuted in the UK charts at No. 5 only a couple of weeks after a German band, NYCC, had seen their (dire) disco-type cover version of 'Fight For Your Right' scaling the Top 20. NYCC's record was, in turn, inspired by one of 1998's biggest selling singles: a remix by New York DJ Jason Nevins of Run DMC's 1983 single 'It's Like That'. That both the Beasties and Run DMC would have Top 5 hits in the UK eleven years after their ill-fated tour seemed inconceivable until it actually happened. And even though Run DMC's No. 1 hit was down to a remix that sped up the original to make it appeal to house music fans, the revival of all things old school provided the atmosphere in which it could work.

The mid-90s saw a resurgence in interest in the early days of rap, with artists and fans alike locking once again into the imperatives that drove the old school pioneers and the mid-80s innovators to fashion hip-hop's most invigorating musical statements. Inspired to look back by the creative bankruptcy of much of what was passing for rap music at the close of the first quarter of the decade, people began to turn once again to the four original elements of the culture. Groups like the Wu-Tang Clan undoubtedly played a part, helping to shift the commercial balance back from the west coast gangsta sound towards rougher beats and sharper rhyme skills, but their unprecedented success alone cannot explain the sheer breadth of the old school revival.

In the increasingly fractured and fragmented music

marketplace of the end of the century, old school hip-hop's core values seem to offer something traditional and fundamental that are worth grabbing hold of. As dance music in particular becomes ever more mechanised the simple act of looping the sounds of a real drummer feels like it's offering a return to a more human time and style of music making. Breakdancing no longer appears to be the hackneyed preserve of clueless advertising directors wishing to spice up the selling of some exceedingly dull product. Instead, the discipline's work ethic and experimentation read like a call to the barricades for anyone who would be creative. The ever more frequent sightings of breakdancers flexing their moves to drum 'n' bass tracks on *Top Of The Pops* reinforce the practice and the philosophies while reminding the viewer that this is an art. Rapping is broadly respected as a skill rather than something you do when you can't sing, and after twenty years of hip-hop the music buying public is undoubtedly better equipped to ascertain who's doing it skillfully and with feeling and who's not. Scratching records is so much a part of the way sounds are made that it has almost reached the point foretold by the pioneers of hip-hop that the turntable is considered an instrument. It was a good time to release an album that incorporates so much of what constitutes real, original, experimental but accessible hip-hop.

And as it had gone back to its roots and left the posturing and negativity of the gangsta sub-genre behind, so progressive, old school-inspired rap began once again to be embraced by fans and makers of alternative rock music. When Public Enemy, Eric B & Rakim and Boogie Down Productions had made waves outside hip-hop in the period between 1986 and 1988, it was usually with the experiment-hungry consumers of so-called 'indie' music; people for whom an attitude and a defiant stand against being force-fed music biz-sponsored pap were key values they looked for in a musician. This is where the vaguely nostalgic nature of the old school renaissance meets the Beasties legacy head on, and where questions of responsibility and influence begin to become blurred.

Beck Hansen, an artist championed by the Beasties, managed by the same Gold Mountain crew and, on his platinum-selling and highly regarded *Odelay* album, produced by the Dust Brothers, is emblematic of a new, post-*Check Your Head* consciousness. Beck incorporates blues and folk idioms into his take on hip-hop: that he's as knowledgeable and enthusiastic about ancient records made on acoustic guitars as he is about hip-hop history is evident throughout *Odelay*, and in this regard he's a singular artist. Yet the embrace he was given by fans of alternative music would have been inconceivable had the Beasties of *Check Your Head* and *Ill Communication* never existed. Beck's success meant that when the old school hip-hop resurrection began, it wasn't just rap fans who took notice. And a world in which Beck is a star is a world in which *Hello Nasty* cannot fail. And as far as the critics were concerned, it didn't. To describe the album as well-received would be a gross understatement. *Hello Nasty* entered the UK album charts at No. 1 on Sunday July 12th 1998, two days before its release in America. It was almost uniformly adored by everyone from teen magazines to tabloids, the music and style press and the daily newspapers, with its ratings never dropping below four out of five in the magazines that adopted marking systems.

Both teen pop magazine *Smash Hits* and adult-oriented rock and film guide *Uncut* made *Hello Nasty* Album Of The Month. "This is blisteringly exciting stuff...Faultless?" asked the latter's reviewer, Michael Bonner. "Guess so." "Classic stuff," opined Dan Cleeve in *Smash Hits*. "With a whole host of hip-hop pretenders cropping up every week the Beastie Boys are back to reclaim their crown!" Dance music monthly *Muzik* found the Beasties "reaching new heights of daring and pulling it off." Frank Tope thought the record "could be their biggest and best trick of all."

The Beasties were "the coolest group in the western world right now," according to *Q*'s Tom Doyle, who felt the album "doesn't mark a massive step in this hugely influential trio's development. But then, in terms of the creative chase, they've already travelled so far and gained so much new ground, the rest are struggling to keep up." Sharon O'Connell, writing in *Melody Maker*, described the record as "another chunky, unutterably funky pot of B-boy bouillabaisse from hip-hop's chief rebel yellers." The Beasties' old mates at *The Sun* concurred, noting that "most of the album sounds as if it was recorded in a space station, but the lyrics are down to earth." *The Sunday Times* called *Hello Nasty* "a highly coherent, carefully paced work, bound together by an irrepressible sense of fun and invention." Writer Andrew Smith concluded by saying the album was "quite wonderful." Caroline Sullivan in *The Guardian* felt moved to describe it as "the perfect party soundtrack by the perfect party band."*Hip-Hop Connection* welcomed the band back into the fold with open arms. Andrew Emery wrote that "*Hello Nasty* is exactly as good as you could wish it to be. This is your first essential purchase of 1998, and only the lowest churl would deny the Beasties their self-bestowed genius. No-one else will ever be able to do what the Beastie Boys do."

In a lengthy and in-depth review in *NME*, John Mulvey saw in the record traces of the same themes of de-personalisation, isolation and pre-millenial unease that informed the benchmark rock album of 1997, Radiohead's *OK Computer*. "Welcome to *Yo Computer*," he suggested drily, "1998's prize take on the daily dystopian nightmare, only with fancy beats and better jokes." He went on to describe the album as "a genre-busting, brain-and-body-stimulating party with conscience" and adroitly places it into the context of the hip-hop renaissance. "Never have they given so much out, never given so much away," he concludes, "And perversely, through *Hello Nasty*, never have they been cleverer, funnier, more radical or more thrilling...there's work to be done, minds to be expanded, planets to be saved." Which, pretty much, is where we came in. The Beastie Boys had come full circle.

CONCLUSION

Back on stage at the Academy, 'Sabotage' has reached the meltdown portion in the middle of the song where all the instruments briefly grind to a halt. Keyboard Money Mark bounds from behind his pianos and breaks into a sprint. He's behind the riser on which Mix Master Mike stands, hands poised to flex over the turntables, by the time Yauch's Larry Graham-style fuzz bass glissando flourish kicks the song's gargantuan riff back into motion. The half whispered chants - "Listen up y'all, this is sabotage" - are gradually gaining volume and intensity as he re-emerges between Yauch and Horovitz on the opposite side of the stage. His momentum looks unstoppable. As the song teeters on the brink of explosion he reaches his keyboards, vaults over one and realises his miscalculation a fraction of a second too late. At exactly the point where every instrument rejoins the riff, Mark's hands land on the keyboard and start wrenching those huge squalls of analogue noise from the ageing machinery. But the rest of his body smashes into his other keyboard, flattening the stand and sending the instrument flying into the pit in between the stage and the crowd. As far as chaos and destruction go, it's remarkably stylish. And as a final image from years of odd behaviour, idiosyncracies and provocative jocularity, it seems curiously fitting.

So what, in the final analysis, do the Beastie Boys actually *mean*? What have they achieved or contributed beyond the (very considerable) obvious? And where do they go from here? I think the answer to the second of these three questions helps inform our responses to the other two: put simply, the musical landscape at the turn of the 21st century would be significantly diminished without the Beasties' presence. Over the years they have played a crucial role in popularising rap music beyond its immediate constituency, and then helped to resuscitate it when the music seemed to be throttling itself in mediocrity. They have shown up the limitations of the Bob Dylan-style wind-em-all-up approach to the media and proved that while it is possible to overestimate the intelligence of your audience you're unlikely ever to do the opposite. They have discovered new ways of making music out of old records, helped proliferate the idea that the popular culture of today is as important and as historic as the revered icons of yesterday and proved that pop and politics *do* mix. Furthermore, they have shown that uncool can be cool, but not all the time, and blasted a space in the popular cultural continuum within which Beck, the Prodigy, Rage Against The Machine, the Mo' Wax label, Cypress Hill, Quentin Tarantino's *Pulp Fiction*, Keyboard Money Mark and many others have been able to operate. For all these things, and their label, their magazine, their tireless campaigning for Tibet and the Freedom Concerts, for their funnier jokes and almost everything they've recorded, we can do little other than salute them.

Yet the most important part of the Beastie Boys story is perhaps the most obvious and fundamental. They have proved that growing up doesn't mean growing old, have shown that moving forward artistically is actually pretty meaningless unless it's backed up with human progress, and have shown that taking a measure of responsibility for your life is something worth aspiring to. In times of chaos and confusion, destruction and depression, the Beastie Boys have lifted us because they know that everyone has the power to change their own life, and once you understand this, there's no limits. That, it seems to me, is both who they really are *and* what they mean; and, as indications of a future go, it's stirring, powerful stuff. Twelve years from their LP debut, the Beastie Boys are bigger, stronger and, unbelievably, actually *better* than ever before. May they remain forever ill.

References

Articles referenced and/or quoted in this work are listed below:

Chapter One

'Indispensible Heroes of Hip-Hop', *NME*, 11th July 1998, by Ted Kessler.

'Rapper's Delight', *Guitar World*, June 1994, by Daniel B Levine.

'The Nature of the Beasties', *Hot Press*, 13th July 1994, by Stuart Clark.

'Beastie Boys II Men', *Newsday*, 12th April 1992, by Frank Owen.

'Licensed To Chill', *DJ Times*, July 1994, by Jim Tremayne.

'Crude Stories, A Day in the Life of the Rudest, Loudest, Deffest, Most Obnoxious Rappers in the World', *Spin*, March 1987, by Tom Cushman and the Beastie Boys. [Note: many of the quotes in this piece are attributed to the band as a whole rather than to the individuals.]

'Mission Impossible', *Dirt* No.1, by Bob Mack.

'Def Jam - A Success Story' by Bill Adler, sleevenotes to Def Jam compilation album *Kick It!*

'From Start To Finish', *Rock and Soul*, October 1987, by Scott Mehno.

'Boys Will Be Boys, And These Will Be Beasties', *Detroit Free Press*, 20th March 1987, by Gary Graff.

'Triumph of the Ill', *Details*, June 1994, by Pat Blashill.

I Make My Own Rules, LL Cool J with Karen Hunter, Ilion Books/St Martin's Press, 1997.

'Beastie Boys - Boy Coastal' by Billy Miller.

'Licensed To Trill', *NME*, 25th April 1992, by James Brown.

'Beast Friends', *Kerrang!*, 19th March 1987, by Stefan Chirazi.

'Growing Pains', *Hip-Hop Connection*, June 1994, by Martin Pearson.

Chapter Two

Beastie Boys interview, *Playboy*, July 1987, by Charles M. Young.
'Men Or Beasties?' *NME*, 11th January 1986, by Don Watson.
'Rap Around The Cock', *NME*, 17th January 1987, by Steven Wells.
'Growing Pains', *Hip-Hop Connection*, ibid.
'Fight For Your Right To...Your Own Clothing Range?' *The Independent On Sunday*, 19th June 1994, by Ben Thompson.
'The Original Nasal Kids', *Xtra*, 8th December 1994, by Joe Clark.

Chapter Three

'Boys Will Be Boys, And These Will Be Beasties', *Detroit Free Press*, ibid.
'Def Jam - A Success Story', sleeve notes to *Kick It!* album, ibid.
'An Interview With Adam Yauch', from *Institute for Labour and Mental Health, Tikkun*, No. 6, Vol.11, interview by Akiba Lerner and Mark LeVine.
The Ice Opinion, as told to Heidi Sigmund, St. Martin's Press 1994.
'A Bad Rep Hangs Over Rapper's Tour', *Detroit Free Press*, 26th July 1987, by John D. Gonzalez.
'From Start To Finish', *Rock And Soul*, ibid.
'Beastie Boys II Men', *Newsday*, ibid.

Chapter Four

'An Interview With Adam Yauch', from *Institute for Labour and Mental Health, Tikkun*, No.6, Vol.11, ibid.

'Moral Panic, the Media and British Rave Culture', printed in *Microphone Fiends: Youth Music & Youth Culture*, edited by Andrew Ross & Tricia Rose, Routledge 1994.

'Eyewitness: The Beastie Boys Invade The UK, May 1987' from *Q*, June 1996, interviews by Howard Johnson.

'Filthy Beasties - Should These Pop Shockers Be Allowed Into Britain?', *The Daily Star*, 15th April 1987, by Ivor Key.

'This Trash Will Harm Our Youth', *The Daily Star*, 15th April 1987, by Liz Phillips.

'Keep Beastie Boys Out Of Britain!' *The News Of The World*, 3rd May 1987, by Annette Witheridge and Mick Hamilton.

'Pop Chiefs Slap Ban On Filthy Beasties!', *The Sun*, 13th May 1987, by Craig MacKenzie.

'Pop Idols Sneer At Dying Kids - Shame of Rampaging Stars', *The Daily Mirror*, 14th May 1987, by Gill Pringle.

'Beastie Boys Go Bonkers - Brawling Rockers in Day of Drunken 4-letter Mayhem', *The Sun*, 14th May 1987, by Craig MacKenzie and Kevin O'Sullivan.

'Keep Out! Fury Over Pop Yobs Who Mocked Dying Kids', *The Daily Mirror*, 15th May 1987, by Gill Pringle.

'Liar! Beasties Rap Charity Woman, Cancer Kids Jibe Denied', *The Sun*, 15th May 1987, by Craig MacKenzie.

'Car-nage As Band Bows Out', *The Sun*, May 15th 1987, no by-line.

'Beasties Back On The Rampage', *The Daily Star*, 15th May 1987, by Geoff Baker.

'Shabby Secrets of the Beastly Beasties', *The Sun*, 15th May 1987, by David Jones.

'Britain Won't Ban The Beasties', *The Daily Mirror*, 16th May 1987, by Graham Barnes.

'Rave Threat To Beasties', *The Sun*, 22nd May 1987, by Garry Bushell.

'Threat To Knife Me', *The Sun*, 25th May 1987, by Garry Bushell.

'Honourable Members', *The Independent*, 26th May 1987, by Dave Hill.

'Boys Will Be Boys, And These Will Be Beasties', *Detroit Free Press*, ibid.

'Beastie Boys Flee As Riot Halts Show', *The News Of The World*, 31st May 1987, by Mike Atchinson.

'Beastie Caged - He Faces Wounding After Riot', *The Daily Star*, 1st June 1987, by Frank Curran.

'Battle Of The Beasties! Riot Terror At Rock Concert', *The Sun*, 1st June 1987, by Garry Bushell.

Chapter Five

'In The Belly Of The Beasties', *NME*, 15th July 1989, by James Brown.

'License Renewed', *Rolling Stone*, 15th June 1989, by Fred Goodman.

'Whatever Happened To The Beastie Boys?', *The Face*, August 1989.

Beastie Boys interview, *Melody Maker*, 5th August 1989, by Ted Mico.

'Beastie Boy Cleared Of Assault', *The Daily Telegraph*, 12th November 1987, no byline.

'Beastie Boy Cleared', *The Times*, 12th November 1987, no byline.

Chapter Six

'"All Aboard the Night Train": Flow, Layering, and Rupture in Post-industrial New York', from *Black Noise: Rap Music and Black Culture in Contemporary America*, Wesleyan University Press/University Press of New England, 1994, by Tricia Rose.

'Still Nasty After All These Years', *Boston Globe*, 3rd November 1989, by Jim Sullivan.

Beastie Boys interview, *Melody Maker*, 5th August 1989, by Ted Mico.

'Who's Deffer? The Beastie Boys and LL Cool J Wrestle For The

Summer's Hip Hop Crown', *Request*, August 1989, by Keith Moerer.

'Whatever Happened To The Beastie Boys?', *The Face*, ibid.

'The Dust Brothers Wrote The Book On A New Type Of Hip-Hop Production, And They're Adding To The Library', *Bay Area Music Magazine*, 6th May 1994, by Nancy Whalen.

'Return Of The Beasties', *Hip-Hop Connection*, August 1989, by Malu Halasa (a slightly different version of this interview appeared in a contemporaneous issue of *Record Mirror*).

'In The Belly Of The Beasties', *NME*, ibid.

'Growing Pains', *Hip-Hop Connection*, ibid.

Album review, *NME*, 29th July 1989, by Roger Morton.

'Cocks Of The Walk', *Melody Maker*, 29th July 1989, by David Stubbs.

'The Beasties: Def, Not Dumb', *Rolling Stone*, 10th August 1989, by David Handelman.

'Still Illin', The Beastie Boys Are Back! Set The Controls To Maximum Snot!', *Q*, August 1989, by Charles Shaar Murray.

'Boys Will Be Beasties', *Time* (US edition), 14th August 1989, by Emily Mitchell.

Album review, *Time*, August 1989, by David Hiltbrand.

'Rude, Lewd And Shamelessly Funny', *The Times*, 22nd July 1989, by David Sinclair.

Album review, *Smash Hits*, 9th August 1989, by Miranda Sawyer.

'Sounds Too Beastly!', *The Daily Mail*, 14th August 1989, by Marcus Berkmann.

Album review, *Hip-Hop Connection*, August 1989, by Nick Smash.

'Bring Me The Head Of Charlton Heston', *NME*, 13th March 1993, by Angus Batey.

Chapter Seven

'Beastie Boys Trying To Beat One-Hit Wonder Rap', *Star*

Tribune, 11th May 1992, by Jon Bream.
'To Live And Get High In LA', *Select*, July 1994, by Adam Higginbotham.
'Breaking The Ground With The Beastie Boys', *Montreal Gazette*, 10th January 1993, by Dave Larsen.
'Licensed To Chill', *DJ Times*, ibid.
'Boys To Men', *Rolling Stone*, 28th May 1992, by Alan Light.
'Success Goes To The Beasties' Head', *Daily News Of Los Angeles*, May 15th 1992, by Bruce Britt.
'Indispensable Heroes Of Hip Hop', *NME*, ibid.
Unknown LA magazine, by Aidin Vaziri.
'When Rap's Great White Hopes Come To Town...', *Pulse!* July 1994 by Michael Jarrett.
'Beastie Boys II Men', *Newsday*, ibid.
'A New Sound, But The Boys Are Still Beastie', *Detroit Free Press*, May 15th 1992, by Gary Graff.
'Beasties Have Their 'Head' Together', *Orlando Sentinel Tribune*, 22nd May 1992, by Parry Gentleman.
'Breaking The Ground With The Beastie Boys', *Montreal Gazette*, ibid.
Album review of *Check Your Head*, *People Weekly*, June 1992, by David Hiltbrand.
'Success Goes To The Beasties' Head', *Daily News Of Los Angeles*, ibid.

Chapter Eight

'Meet The Prez: Mike D Takes Charge', *Swill*, August 1993, by Bruce Wheeler.
Lies Lies Lies issue 5, 1992, by Angus Batey and Ed Stern.
'New York, New York', *Dirt*, by Spike Jonze.
'Mike D's Finance Seminar', *Dirt* No. 4, 1993, by Mike D.
'Triumph Of The Ill', *Details*, June 1994, by Pat Blashill.
'Rapper's Delight', *Guitar World*, ibid.
'Beastie Boy Yauch Pledges To Hold Concert Until Tibet Is

Free', *Addicted To Noise* (http://www.addict.com), 22nd September 1997, by Gil Kaufman.

'MC Adam Yauch: Check His Head', *Shambhala Sun*, January 1995, by Amy Yuill Green, Jerry Granelli and J. Anthony Granelli.

'Beastie Boys: Boy-Coastal', by Billy Miller.

'The Making Of The Tibetan Freedom Concert', *Addicted To Noise*, by Kathy Mancall.

'From Beastie To Buddha', Metal Hammer, 1994, by Ian Winwood.

Chapter Nine

'Always On Vacation? At Home And On The Road With The Beastie Boys', *Grand Royal 1*, 1993, by Bob Mack.

'Beastie Boys: Boy-Coastal', by Billy Miller, ibid.

'Rapper's Delight', *Guitar World*, ibid.

'Recording On The Fly', *Mix*, June 1994, by Adam Beyda.

'New York, New York', *Dirt*, by Spike Jonze.

'When Rap's Great White Hope Comes To Your Town...' *Pulse!*, ibid.

'The Making Of The Tibetan Freedom Concert', *Addicted To Noise*, ibid.

'Deaf Jams', *NME*, 23rd March 1996, by Johnny Cigarettes.

Chapter Ten

'Indispensible Heroes Of Hip Hop', *NME*, ibid.

News item, *NME*, December 1997, no byline.

Chat item, *America On Line*, 1997, no byline.

'Boyzgrown', *Uncut*, August 1998, by Michael Bonner.

Album review, *Muzik*, August 1998, by Frank Tope.

'Style Counsellors', *Q*, August 1998, by Tom Doyle.

'D'You Know What, They're Mean!', *Melody Maker*, 11th July 1998, by Sharon O'Connell.

Album review, *The Sun*, 6th July 1998, no byline.

'Record Of The Week', *The Sunday Times*, 5th July 1998, by Andrew Smith.

'Beast Masters', *The Guardian*, 3rd July 1998, by Caroline Sullivan.

Album Review, *Hip Hop Connection*, August 1998, by Andrew Emery.

'Hello 'Hello' Good To Be Back', *NME*, 4th July 1998, by John Mulvey.

Unless stated otherwise, all quotes from Bill Adler, Charlie Ahearn, Fab 5 Freddy, Kool Herc, Joseph 'Run' Simmons and Chris Stein are from interviews with the author, 1998.

Discography

Any Beastie Boys discography has to contend with the problems posed by multiple formats, DJ promo releases, different track availability in different territories and the general proliferation of singles. The following concise discography is not an attempt to be exhaustive and definitive, but should enable the collector to find every track the Beasties have recorded and released officially. Therefore many items such as promos, white labels and different formats have not been included, unless they include tracks unavailable elsewhere. Where possible a note has been made of album availability of non-album material (eg: several Japanese versions of the band's albums contain B-sides). Except where noted, all catalogue numbers are for UK releases.

ALBUMS

Licensed To Ill
November 1986, Def Jam
Def Jam 4500621
Produced by Rick Rubin and Beastie Boys
Rhymin And Stealin/It's The New Style/She's Crafty/Posse In Effect/Slow Ride/Girls/Fight For Your Right/No Sleep Till Brooklyn/Paul Revere/Hold It Now, Hit It/Brass Monkey/ Slow And Low/Time To Get Ill

Paul's Boutique
July 1989, Capitol Records
EST 2102
CD EST2102
Produced by Beastie Boys, Dust Brothers, Mario G. Caldato Jr.
To All The Girls.../Shake Your Rump/Johnny Ryall/Egg Man/ High Plains Drifter/The Sounds Of Science/3-Minute Rule/ Hey Ladies/5 Piece Chicken Dinner/Looking Down The Barrel Of A Gun/Car Thief/What Comes Around/Shadrach/ Ask For Janice/B-Boy Bouillabaisse [a) 59 Chrystie Street b) Get On The Mic c) Stop That Train d) Year And A Day e) Hello Brooklyn f) Dropping Names g) Lay It On Me h) Mike On The Mic i) A.W.O.L.]

Japanese version includes the following extra tracks:
33% God/Dis Yourself In '89 (Just Do It)

Check Your Head
April 1992, Grand Royal/Capitol Records
EST 2171
CD EST2171
Produced by Beastie Boys, Mario Caldato Jr.
Jimmy James/Funky Boss/Pass The Mic/Gratitude/Lighten Up/Finger
Lickin' Good/So What'cha Want/The Biz vs The Nuge/Time For
Livin'/Something's Got To Give/The Blue Nun/Stand
Together/Pow!/The Maestro/Groove Holmes/ Live At P.J.'s/Mark On
The Bus/Professor Booty/In 3's/ Namaste

Japanese version includes the following extra tracks: Dub The Mic
(Instrumental)/Drunken Praying Mantis Style/Pass The Mic (Pt.2, Skills To
Pay The Bills)/Netty's Girl

Some Old Bullshit
February 1994 Grand Royal
EST 2877
CD EST 89843
Produced by: Various
Egg Raid On Mojo (4 track)/Beastie Boys/Transit Cop/Jimi/ Holy
Snappers/Riot Fight/Ode To.../Michelle's Farm/Egg Raid On Mojo/
Transit Cop (4 track)/Cooky Puss/Bonus Batter/ Beastie
Revolution/Cooky Puss (Censored Version)

Ill Communication
June 1994, Grand Royal/Capitol Records
EST 2290
CD EST2290
Produced by Beastie Boys, Mario Caldato Jr.
Sure Shot/Tough Guy/B-Boys Makin' With The Freak Freak/ Bobo On The
Corner/Root Down/Sabotage/Get It Together/ Sabrosa/The Update/
Futterman's Rule/Alright, Hear This/ Eugene's Lament/Flute Loop/Do
It/Ricky's Theme/Heart Attack Man/The Scoop/Shambala/Bodhisattva
Vow/Transitions

An interesting oddity: A small number of US CDs were mis-pressed, containing a Jon Secada album instead of the Beasties.

An American promo version exists with 'clean' (swear words removed) versions of all tracks.

Japanese version includes the following extra tracks: Dope Little Song/Resolution Time/Mullet Head/The Vibes

The In Sound From Way Out!
Grand Royal/Capitol Records
1996
EST 33590
Groove Holmes/Sabrosa/Namaste/Pow/Son Of Neckbone/ In 3's/ Eugene's Lament/Bobo On The Corner/Shambala/Lighten Up/Ricky's Theme/Transitions/Drinkin' Wine

Hello Nasty
July 1998, Grand Royal/Capitol Records
EST 495723 2
CD EST 495723 2
Produced by Beastie Boys and Mario Caldato Jr.
Super Disco Breakin'/The Move/Remote Control/Song For The Man/Just A Test/Body Movin'/Intergalactic/Sneakin' Out The Hospital/Putting Shame In Your Game/Flowin' Prose/And Me/Three Mc's And One DJ/Can't, Won't, Don't Stop/Song For Junior/I Don't Know/The Negotiation Limerick File/Electrify/Picture This/Unite/Dedication/Dr. Lee, PhD/Instant Death

The following tracks are believed to exist and may appear on future B-sides: Boo Boo/Attitude Boy/Mike Phone/Silly/ Another Dimension/Frankie/Space Shit/Kalimba/Piano Joint/Frankie 2/Basketball Raw/Tribesman/Iced Coffee/ Pucho/End/Listen/Evil Shit/If I Could Fly/I'm Not Fueling It/My People/Arp Shit

Japanese version includes the following extra track: Slow And Low (Mix Master Mike Remix Version)

US version has Can't Won't Don't Stop retitled as The Grasshopper Unit (Keep Movin')

SINGLES/EPs

Polly Wog Stew EP
1982 Ratcage
7" MOTR21
12" MOTR 21T
Beastie Boys/Transit Cop/Jimi/Holy Snappers/Riot Fight/ Ode To.../
Michelle's Farm/Egg Raid On Mojo

Cookie Puss EP
1983 Ratcage
12" MOTR26
Produced by Dug Pomeroy and Beastie Boys
Cookie Puss/Bonus Batter/Beastie Revolution/Cookie Puss (Censored Version)
Note: The disc actually lists title as Cookie Puss while the sleeve has the spelling Cooky Puss.

Rock Hard
1984 Def Jam
12" Def Jam 002
Rock Hard/Beastie Groove/Party's Getting Rough/Beastie Groove (Instrumental)

She's On It
1986 Def Jam
7" Def Jam A6686
12" Def Jam TA6686
She's On It/Slow And Low

Hold It Now, Hit It
1986 Def Jam
7" Def Jam A7055
12" Def Jam TA7055
Hold It Now, Hit It/Acapulco (Hold It Now, Hit It Accapella)

Fight For Your Right
1986 Def Jam
12" Def Jam 650 353 C
Fight For Your Right/Girls
The Australian, Dutch and some US versions included the following extra tracks: She's On It (Extended Mix)/Paul Revere

The UK version included the following extra tracks: No Sleep Till Brooklyn/She's On It/Time To Get Ill

She's Crafty
1986 Def Jam
12" Def Jam 650498 6
She's Crafty/No Sleep Till Brooklyn

It's The New Style
1986 Def Jam
12" Def Jam 6581696
7" Def Jam 6581697
It's The New Style/Paul Revere/It's The New Style (Instrumental)/Paul Revere (Instrumental)

No Sleep Till Brooklyn
1987 Def Jam
7" Beast 1
Limited Crashed plane picture disc 12" Beast P1
12" Beast P1
No Sleep Till Brooklyn/She's Crafty

Girls
September 1987 Def Jam
7" Beast 3
7" Fold out picture sleeve edition Beast 3
7" Beasties go X rated sleeve Beast Q3
12" Beasties go X rated sleeve Beast TQ3
Girls/She's Crafty/Rock Hard

Love American Style EP
July 1989 Capitol
12" 12CL540
CD CDCL 540
Hey Ladies/Shake Your Rump/33% God/Dis Yourself In '89 (Just Do It)
7" (Love Mexican Style EP) CL540
Hey Ladies/Shake Your Rump

An Exciting Evening At Home With Shadrach, Meshach and Abednego EP
October 1990 Capitol
12" V15523
Shadrach/Caught In The Middle Of A 3-Way Mix/And What You Give Is What You Get/Car Thief/Some Dumb Cop Gave Me Two Tickets Already

Pass The Mic
April 1992 Capitol
7" CL653
12" 12CL653
12" 12CL653A
CD CL653
Cass 4V 15816
Pass The Mic/Pass The Mic (Pt. 2 Skills To Pay Bills)/Professor Booty/
Time For Livin'

So What'cha Want
1992 Capitol
12" Y15847
CD C2-15847
Hey Ladies/So What'cha Want

Jimmy James
1992 Capitol
12" Y 15836
CD C2-15836
Cass 4V-15836
Jimmy James (Single Version)/The Maestro/Jimmy James/Boomin'
Granny/Jimmy James (Original Original Version)/Drinkin' Wine

Frozen Metal Head EP
1992 Capitol
12" CL665
CD CL665
12" Picture Disk 12CLS 665
Jimmy James/The Blue Nun/Jimmy James (Original Original Version)/
Drinkin' Wine

Gratitude EP
1992 Capitol
12" Y 0777 7 1595165
CD V2 0777 7 15944 27
Gratitude/Stand Together (Live At French's Tavern, Sydney,
Australia)/Finger Lickin' Good (Government Cheese Remix)/Gratitude
(Live At Budokan)/Honkey Rink

Get It Together/Sabotage
June 1994 Capitol
7" CL716

CD GD CL 716
10″ 10CL 716
CD C2 7243 58171 20
12″ Y 7243 8 58185 6 1
Cass 4 V 7243 A 58171 44
Get It Together/Sabotage/Dope Little Song

Sure Shot
1994 Capitol
7″ 7243 8 81734 7 6
12″ 7243 8 58226 1 2
Sure Shot/Mullet Head/Son Of Neck Bone/Sure Shot (Nardone mix)

Root Down EP
1995 Grand Royal/Capitol
12″ GR108
CD Capitol CDP 7243 8 33603 2 1
Root Down (Clean Version)/Ricky's Theme (Clean Version)

Aglio E Olio EP
1995, Grand Royal/Capitol
12″ GR026
CD CDGRO26
Brand New/Deal With It/Believe Me/Nervous Assistant/Square Wave In
Unison/You Caught A Bad One/I Can't Think Straight/I Want Some

Japanese version includes the following extra track: Soba Violence
Australian version includes the following extra track: Soba Violence/Light
My Fire

Intergalactic
1998 Grand Royal/Capitol
12″ CL803
CD CDCL803
Intergalatic/Intergalatic (Prisoners Of Technology /TMS 1 Remix)/
Intergalatic (Fuzzy Logic Remix)/Hail Sagan (Special K)

The European release and the US release have different artwork for the
same single.

VIDEOS

The Beastie Boys Video
1987, CBS/FOX
38 mins
VHS
Rhymin And Stealin/Fight For Your Right/Hold It Now, Hit It/No Sleep
Till Brooklyn/She's On It/She's Crafty

Sabotage Video
1994, Capitol Video
An Ari Macropoulos and Nathanial Hornblower Film
59 minutes.
VHS
Sabotage/Djembe/Gratitude (Live)/Sabotage (Uncut Video)/The
Hurricane Freestyle/Triphammer/The Skills To Pay The Bills (Original
Version)/Time For Livin' (Live)/Sabrosa/Something's Got To
Give/Screaming At A Wall (Live)/Namaste (Live)/Futterman's Rule/5
Piece Chicken Dinner/Jimmy James/Conga And Bass/Mullet
Head/Ricky's Theme/So What'cha Want (Live With Cypress Hill)

The Skills To Pay The Bills Video
1992, Capitol Video
Directed by Nathanial Hornblower except where indicated
40 minutes
VHS/LD/DVD,
Looking Down The Barrel Of A Gun/So What'cha Want (Single
Version)/Netty's Girl/Shake Your Rump (Video Version)/Egg Raid On
Mojo (Directed By Phillip Pucci)/Shadrach (Mosh Version) Live and
Unreleased/Holy Snappers/Hey Ladies (Directed By Adam
Bernstein)/Slow And Low (Live)/Pass The Mic (Video Version)/Ask For
Janice, Pt. II/Shadrach (Abstract Impressionist Version)

COMPILATIONS
The following is a selection of tracks that appear on various artist albums.

In Defense Of Animals, Volume 2
Caroline
Son Of A Neck Bone

(Biz Markie) Best Of Unreleased Biz Bootleg LP
Groove Holmes (Live vs. the Biz)

Bored Generation
Epitaph Records
Nervous Assistant

Clueless Soundtrack
1996, EMD/Capitol Records
Mullet Head

Def Jam Classics, Vol 1
PGD/Polygram/Def Jam
Fight For Your Right
Rhymin and Stealin

Def Jam Greatest Hits
PGD/Polygram/Def Jam
Brass Monkey

Def Jam Greatest Hits: Hardcore
PGD/Polygram/Def Jam
Paul Revere

Def Jam Music Group 10th Box Set
PGD/Polygram/Def Jam
Hold It Now, Hit It/Paul Revere/No Sleep Till Brooklyn/Brass
Monkey/Fight For Your Right

Headz 2a/2b
1996, Mo Wax/A&M Records
Bodhisattva Vow (Instrumental)/Flute Loop (Instrumental)

Heart Of Soul
Columbia Records
Fight For Your Right

Jerky Boys Soundtrack
Four Fly Guys

Keep It Slammin'
The Skills To Pay The Bills

Kickin' Da Flava
EMI

Get It Together (Buck Wild Remix Clean Version)

Def Jam: Kick It!
Def Jam
Rock Hard

Kool Rap
Priority Records
No Sleep Till Brooklyn

Matra Mix
1996, Mushroom Records
Shambala

Grand Royal Mixed Drink
Grand Royal Records
Featuring Adrock on the DJ Hurricane track, Stick 'Em Up, (CB4/Grand
Royal Mixed Drink Version)

M.O.M.O: Music For Our Mother Ocean
UNI/Interscope Records
Netty's Girl

No Alternative
1993, Arista Records
It's The New Style (Live)

New York Thrash
Roir Records
Riot Fight/B.E.A.S.T.I.E. Go

Rap The Beat
Fight For Your Right

Rap's Biggest Hits
K-Tel
Fight For Your Right

Rap: Most Valuable Players
K-Tel
Hey Ladies

Rap Rap Rap
K-Tel Records
Paul Revere

Rap Declares War
Rhino
Slow Ride

Rebirth Of Cool, Volume 3
PGD/Fourth & Broadway
Get It Together

Speed Trials
1984, Homestead Records
Egg Raid On Mojo (Live)

Strikeforce, Volume 1
Fight For Your Right

Tibetan Freedom Concert
1997, Grand Royal/Capitol Records
Root Down (Live w/It's The New Style Intro)

X Games, Volume 1
1997, Tommy Boy
Fight For Your Right

X-Mix Records Fall Sampler Vol. 21
1994, X-Mix Records
Get It Together (Armand's 2% Phat Mix)

INTERVIEW DISCS

Several are available, including: Blender CD-ROM-Mag Volume 1.4/2.5, 1995, Felix Dennis, Denis Publishing; Def and Dumb, 1996, Feedback; The Interview 1997, Baktabak/Tabak Marketing; Interview Picture Disk, 1987, Baktabak/Tabak Marketing.

SIDE PROJECTS

Drum Machine
1985 Def Jam
MCA and Burzootie
12" Def Jam004
Drum Machine/Drum Machine (Mini Jerk Edit)/Drum Machine (Psycho Dust Version)

Nighty-9: Grand Royal Mixed Drink No.2
Yauch play bass on this Nighty-9 track.
Jhompa

Abstract Rude: Unreleased Grand Royal LP
Yauch plays bass on this officially unreleased track.
OG Crew

Ben Lee: Something To Remember Me By
Mike D. plays drums on this Ben Lee track.
2 Sisters

Björk: Army Of Me Single
1995, Polygram Music
Mike D. Remix under the name A.B.A. Allstars.
Army Of Me (A.B.A. All-Stars Mix),
Army Of Me (Instrumental A.B.A. All-Stars Mix)

BS2000: BS2000
1996, Grand Royal/Capitol Records
An Adrock and AWOL joint experimental album.

DFL: My Crazy Life
1994, Grand Royal Records
Featuring Adrock on bass.
GR002

The Purple Panthers: Germs Tribute Album
Featuring Mike D. on lead vocals.
Now I Hear The Laughter

Big Fat Love: Hellhouse
1997, Grand Royal Records
Produced by Yauch, and Featuring Mike D. on drums in the first seven tracks, originally recorded in 1983.
Cold Rail/Promised Land/Trashman/Evil/Farm Boy From Hell/Mississippi Red/When You're Gonna Get Home

DJ Hurricane: The Hurra
1994, Grand Royal Records
Elbow Room/Four Fly Guys/Elbow Room (Clean Version)/Four Fly Guys (Clean Version)

Jon Spencer Blues Explosion!: Expermental Remixes EP
1995, Matador Records
Mike D and Beck two part remix.
Flavor (Part 1)/Flavor (Part 2)

Milk: Never Dated LP
Adrock on vocals.
SPAM

DJ Hurricane: Severe Damage
1997, Wiiija Records
Adrock co-produced the listed track. Also, the listed UK release has a bonus instrumental album as a promo.
Japanese Eyes/Japanese Eyes (instrumental)

Cibo Matto: Super Relax EP
1997, Warner Bros. Reocrds
Mike D on the mic, according to the liner notes.
Sugar Water (Mike D./Russell Simins/Mario Caldato Jr. Remix)

Ween: Freedom Of '76 Single
1995, Flying Nun Records
Mike D and Mario remix.
Spirit of '76 (Shaved Dog Mix)

Yoko Ono: Rising Mixes EP
1996, Capitol Records
Yauch remix under the name of the A.B.A. Allstars.
The Source (A.B.A. Allstars)

(The Young and the Useless) Real Men Don't Floss EP
Young and Useless/P.M.H./The Wave/Homeboy/Rise and Shine/Funky
Music

Thanks to the following people who helped compile the discography:
Nicholas Campbell (campbeln@isontheweb.com), Co-Lead Discography
Design/Curator of the Beastie Shrine, Brian Chambers (AstroBBoy,
bboy@one.net.au), Co-Lead Discography Design/Artwork Scan Lackey,
Mark Laudenschlager (mdl4424@silver.sdsmt.edu), Rare Recording
Acquisition Specialist.
   A much more in-depth version of the discography published here can be
found on their web site at: http://isontheweb.com/beastiality

INTERNET

The official Beastie Boys web site is exhaustive and regularly updated.
Huge lists of articles, a massive discography and numerous other
interesting facts and figures are available at www.beastieboys.com

There are scores of unofficial Beastie sites also available.